THE LENTEN COOKBOOK

The Lenten Cookbook

Printed in the United States of America.

All information in this book has been provided by or through the contributing authors, reviewed, and verified for accuracy to best ability, knowledge, and belief. Neither the authors nor the publishers are responsible for any errors or omissions. This book and all contents are provided without warranty or representation of any kind.

Contributing Authors

David Geisser

Scott Hahn

Photographs

Roy Matter

Editorial Consultant

Carolyn McKinney

Editors

Anna Maria Dube

Nora Malone

Cover and Interior Design

Perceptions Design Studio

SOPHIA
INSTITUTE PRESS

Sophia Institute Press®
Box 5284, Manchester, NH 03108
1-800-888-9344

www.SophiaInstitute.com
Sophia Institute Press® is a registered trademark of Sophia Institute.

ISBN: 978-1-64413-469-6

Library of Congress Control Number:
2021947798
2nd Printing

THE
Lenten
COOKBOOK

Recipes by
DAVID GEISSER

with essays by
SCOTT HAHN

SOPHIA INSTITUTE PRESS
Manchester, New Hampshire

Contents

Breakfast

Soup

Salad

Collations (Small Meals)

THE LENTEN COOKBOOK

The Joy of Fasting

AN INTRODUCTION

You may not know the name Irma Rombauer, but there's a good chance you've eaten a meal she designed. Mrs. Rombauer was a celebrated hostess in Saint Louis high society until the untimely death of her husband in 1930. Faced with a desperate financial situation, alongside the void left by her spouse, she made a surprising decision: Irma Rombauer wrote a cookbook.

The Joy of Cooking, originally self-published in 1931, went on to become the best-selling American cookbook in history. Today it is in its ninth edition, with more than eighteen million copies sold. Although most home cooks are familiar with the later cover design, with the oversized word "joy" in lowercase letters, the first edition included religious imagery: St. Martha, patron saint of cooks, slaying a dragon (for some reason) with a broom.

What made Mrs. Rombauer's cookbook so successful? The answer is right in the title: She restored joy to preparing food for one's family and guests.

Cookbooks at the time were generally fussy and complicated, often full of fancy restaurant dishes that required techniques and ingredients that weren't readily available to middle-class Americans. Cooking had developed along two tracks: elegance for the elite and just the basics for everyone else. Irma Rombauer taught generations of Americans (including Julia Child, who learned from *The Joy of Cooking*) that delicious and beautiful home-cooked meals were within their reach.

In other words, she highlighted a basic truth about the good life: Sharing our homes, talents, and food with others is a joy-filled part of living well that should be available to everyone. And through her simple recipes and witty commentary, she did her part to make it possible.

So why are we talking about a book of hearty meals and decadent desserts at the beginning of a fasting cookbook? The truth is that the Catholic practice of fasting has come to a somewhat similar place as American cooking in the 1930s. On the one hand, there's the spiritual elite, mostly monks and nuns, who fast regularly and seriously, and on the other hand, there's everybody else, for whom fasting feels like an extreme practice that has fallen into disuse.

The book you are reading comes at what I believe is the beginning of a joyful rediscovery of the Church's traditional disciplines *for everyone*—and, God willing, it will help to push that movement forward. We are finding once again that fasting, and prayerful self-restraint in food choices generally, doesn't have to be either monastic or a few-times-a-year imposition, but it can be part of the everyday arsenal for spiritual growth (and warfare) available to every Christian.

Further, we are rediscovering what so many generations of Christians before us knew: Fasting is part of the good life, and fasting is joyful. As we will see, the testimony of two thousand years of saints and Catholic tradition can lead to no other conclusion. The joy of fasting can be described in many ways, but ultimately, they all come back to a single truth: In denying ourselves the satisfaction of our bodily appetites, we become more aware of, and closer to, the spiritual reality of God.

But let's start before the beginning of the Christian era and explore the practice of fasting in the Old Testament and beyond.

An Ancient Practice

"Yet even now," says the Lord, "return to me with all your heart, with fasting, with weeping, and with mourning; and rend your hearts and not your garments" (Joel 2:12–13).

Fasting wasn't invented by Christians (or Jews, for that matter) but is a universal human practice that the Lord and His Church have sanctified. Periodic, self-imposed limitations on food are attested in just about every culture as a means of supplicating or appeasing angry gods. We see it even in today's secular culture, but the gods are those of health and wellness rather than wind and rain.

As with many (though certainly not all) pagan practices, we see glimmers of true religion in these rituals. Fasting does improve our relationship with the divine, but it's the loving, triune God of the Bible, not the cranky, manmade gods of ancient times, or even the gods of fitness, to whom we must dedicate our sacrifices.

That is, ultimately, what fasting is: a sacrifice. And sacrifice is essential to worship, which is, in turn, the pinnacle duty of the virtue of religion. By "religion," we mean the justice that we owe to God as our Creator, Sustainer, and Redeemer—a debt that we can never repay but can approximate by offering the very best of ourselves to Him. One of the ways we do this is by relinquishing something that we value highly, such as our comfort and freedom from hunger, and offering it to the Lord.

Ultimately, fasting is a sacrifice that is essential to worship. We approximate the debt to which we owe God by offering the very best of ourselves to Him.

Here's how Dag Tessore, author of a beautiful little book on fasting to which we will return throughout these reflections, describes sacrifice in Scripture: "God commanded ... sacrifices to see if man believed in him, or if he was capable of doing something *that makes sense only if God exists*."[1] This, as we will see, distinguishes *fasting* from *healthy eating* or *dieting*: Are we truly sacrificing and offering it to God? Does it make sense only for His sake?

This is what we see in the quotation from the book of the prophet Joel above. Fasting was part of a collection of penances the Israelites would take upon themselves to atone for sins or to beg a favor or pardon from the Lord. Fasting, which mortifies our appetite for food, appears along sackcloth (mortifying our appetite for comfort) and ashes (mortifying our appetite for admiration) several times in the Old Testament. Together, they amount to a renunciation of the temporary goods of this world in favor of the eternal good of the world to come.

This is why the Lord tells His prophet, "Rend your hearts and not your garments." Whatever good these penitential practices might do in terms of this world—maybe fasting sheds a few extra pounds and sackcloth, who knows, exfoliates?—is irrelevant to their spiritual value. Fasting, as a spiritual discipline, is much more about the heart than about the stomach.

And so we read in the book of Jonah that the city of Nineveh repented after the prophet delivered God's judgment. The king announced: "Let neither man nor beast, herd nor flock, taste anything; let them not feed, or drink water, but let man and beast be covered with sackcloth, and let them cry mightily to God" (Jonah 3:7–8). Calling upon the name of the Lord is an essential act of faithfulness in the Old Testament, and it is magnified and sealed by the sacrifice of food and comfort made by the citizens of the city.

And in the book of Ezra, that prophet writes:

Then I proclaimed a fast there, at the river Ahava, that we might humble ourselves before our God, to seek from him a straight way for ourselves, our children, and all our goods. For I was ashamed to ask the king for a band of soldiers and horsemen to protect us against the enemy on our way; since we had told the king, "The hand of our God is for good upon all that seek him, and the power of his wrath is against all that forsake him." So we fasted and besought our God for this, and he listened to our entreaty. (Ezra 8:21–23)

---

[1] Dag Tessore, *Fasting*, trans. Frank Johnson (Hyde Park, NY: New City Press, 2008), 25, emphasis added.

4

Ezra, leading the Israelites home to Jerusalem, proclaimed a fast, demonstrating that physical liberation from captivity was not enough; they needed to be further purified, spiritually, to take up the duties of the People of God in Jerusalem once again.

The Didache recommended weekly fasting on Wednesdays and Fridays, continuing the twice-weekly fasting from the Jewish tradition but shifting the days to commemorate the betrayal of Judas and the Passion of Our Lord.

At this time, Ezra was leading the Israelites home to Jerusalem from their exile in Babylon. The fast demonstrated to his people that physical liberation from captivity was not enough; they needed to be further purified, spiritually, to be ready to take up the duties of the People of God in Jerusalem once again. Further, we see again how fasting magnifies the efficacy of prayer by coupling it to a sacrifice that is a physical act of faith in the Lord.

It was in this context, in which fasting was understood as a prayerful and spiritually purifying sacrifice to the Lord, that the first Christians took up the practice.

Fasting for the First Christians

Early Christian fasting served several purposes: a demonstration of ethical sincerity (e.g., saving food to give as an offering for the needy…); a sign of authentic repentance both before and during penance; preparation for significant religious moments, such as baptism, eucharist, or ordinations; and a symbol of identification with the passion of Christ.[2]

The practice of fasting is attested in the very earliest documents of early Christianity and is unanimously recommended by the Church Fathers. For instance, the first-century *Didache*, the earliest known description of Christian teaching and discipline, says in its very first paragraph: "Bless those who curse you, and pray for your enemies, and *fast for those who persecute you*" (emphasis added). This describes fasting as vicarious expiation for the sins of others.

But that's only one of several references to fasting in the *Didache*. The document recommends that everyone involved in a Baptism should fast for one or two days before the sacrament, and it also encourages weekly fasting on Wednesdays and Fridays. This latter suggestion was meant to continue the habit of twice-weekly fasting from the Jews but to distinguish the followers of Christ by shifting the days from Monday and Thursday to Wednesday and Friday, the former commemorating the betrayal of Judas and the latter the Passion of Our Lord.[3]

---

[2] E. Glenn Hinson, *The Encyclopedia of Early Christianity*, ed. Everett Ferguson, Michael P. McHugh, and Frederick W. Norris, 2nd ed., vol. 1 (New York: Garland Publishing, 1998), 422–423.

[3] Tessore, *Fasting*, 39. Twice-weekly Friday and Saturday fasts eventually came to dominate in the Western Church, though to varying degrees in different times and places. The last vestiges of the Saturday fast weren't officially removed from Canon Law until the Second Vatican Council.

Now, what did it mean to fast in the first centuries of the Church? The truth is that practices varied widely from place to place and even from year to year, as bishops and everyday Christians tried to apply the tradition of fasting to the new reality of Christ and His Church. Tessore writes that one thing is clear, though: By today's standards, all of the diverse fasting regulations were "serious, austere, and demanding." He continues:

> In the early Latin Church, . . . all the faithful, clergy and lay people, fasted. For example, during Lent, for approximately forty days, they ate one meal a day, and that after Vespers. And for the whole of Lent they abstained, not only from eating meat, but also from milk and dairy products and eggs, as well as often from fish, wine and oil.[4]

We will return later to the topic of the invention of Lent, but here we can say that fasting was meant to be not a minor inconvenience but a real sacrifice. It was meant to be not merely a gentle reminder of but also a painful participation in the suffering of Christ.

For this reason, fasting before Easter is also attested in the earliest days of the Church, beginning with Good Friday, then expanding to Holy Week and, ultimately, to a forty-day period before the celebration of the Resurrection. In this, we can see all the meanings of fasting mentioned above rolled into one great fast: frugality for almsgiving, repentance, preparation, and imitation of Christ.

Although there has never been complete uniformity in the Church with regard to fasting—the question of Wednesday versus Saturday fasts was the topic of the quip of St. Ambrose that comes down to us as "when in Rome, do as the Romans do"[5]—the general structure of Christian fasting took shape in the fourth century. It was then that the Council of Nicaea defined the season of Lent, and other customs of weekly fasts and preparations for sacraments settled into near-universal practices.[6]

---

[4] Tessore, *Fasting*, 35–36. These Lenten practices are maintained in law in many Eastern churches, Catholic and Orthodox, to this day, but they are followed by a small minority of the faithful.

[5] Tessore, *Fasting*, 101.

[6] See E. Glenn Hinson, "Fasting," *The Encyclopedia of Early Christianity*, ed. Everett Ferguson, Michael P. McHugh, and Frederick W. Norris, 2nd ed., vol. 1 (New York: Garland Publishing, 1998), 422–423.

The Golden Age of Christendom

Fasting is useful as atoning for and preventing sin, and as raising the mind to spiritual things. And everyone is bound by the natural dictate of reason to practice fasting as far as it is necessary for these purposes.[7]

The Middle Ages saw the development of a comprehensively Christian civilization in Europe. For the vast majority of people, the teachings and disciplines of the Church went without saying and were integrated into the structures and institutions of everyday life. Fasting was no exception.

As with the institutionalization of the virtue of religion in all times and places, this bore astounding fruits—but it also introduced new risks and temptations. The rhythm of fasts and feasts came to be a defining feature of medieval life, uniting the spiritual and the embodied natures of the human person in a complete civilization of faith.

During these centuries, the disintegration of modern life that we take for granted would have been incomprehensible. The idea that there are spheres of life, such as politics and other public matters, that religion could not influence would have been met with a blank stare. The idea that we should pray in private but not in public would have sounded like madness. The idea that the drama of the Gospels and of salvation history is a relic of the past and needn't be recreated in enormous processions and grand feasts and austere fasts would have been seen not just as nonsensical, but as incredibly lame.

Medieval life was hard, to be sure. But, despite popular modern depictions, it wasn't constant, horrific drudgery. In fact, it was precisely because the work of the common serf—and even of the richer classes—was so hard that the rhythm of fasting and feasting became so deeply rooted. It's easier to till the fields day after day when you know that indulgent celebrations of Easter or St. Martin's Day or the Nativity of St. John the Baptist are right around the corner.

And the fasts—Lent and Advent and Ember Days and Rogation Days and so on—formed an essential part of this rhythm of life. These fasts provided the physical lows that made the highs of the feasts all the more celebratory. And of course, those physical lows were often spiritual highs in themselves, as St. Thomas describes above.

---

[7] St. Thomas Aquinas, *Summa theologiae* II-II, Q. 147, art. 3.

But this kind of institutionalization also came with downsides. The rather strict and standardized rules of fasting allowed for some clever workarounds, and the very institution that set the rules bent them for other purposes. Most notably, the rules of abstinence for Lent, which included prohibitions on all land-animal-derived products and not just meat, would be suspended for individuals, families, or regions in recognition of services rendered to the papacy. Soon, these "dispensations" became more the norm than the exception.

Perhaps the most infamous example of using the Church's fasts for other ends is the "Butter Tower" of Rouen Cathedral in France. One of the most spectacular gothic churches of the Middle Ages (or any age), Rouen is a high point of Christian civilization, representing the spiritual grandeur of the Faith in physical form. But its glorious southwest tower was funded by dispensations, sold to wealthy patrons, to eat butter and milk during Lent. That's not exactly the spirit of fasting articulated by the Church Fathers or by St. Thomas Aquinas.

But we shouldn't become obsessed with listing the abuses of medieval fasting disciplines. In a real sense, these disciplines helped to sustain the golden age of Christendom with both their spiritual power and their ability to bring the drama of salvation history to life for every member of the Body of Christ, lay or cleric, peasant or lord, young person or old.

Fasting and Liturgy

As fasting was an act of conversion to God, of purification of the body and the mind, and being in every sense a "good work," it soon became the norm to observe of short or long duration, in preparation for the great Christian feasts.[8]

Christian fasting has always had a liturgical element: That is, fasting disciplines have been pegged to particular days or seasons of the liturgical year and are meant to be shared by entire Christian communities rather than invented by individuals to meet their own needs. In a later essay, we will discuss the challenges of rediscovering the ancient traditions of fasting in an age when many of these disciplines have lapsed.

---

[8] Tessore, *Fasting*, 43.

The famous "Butter Tower" of Rouen Cathedral in France was funded by dispensations, sold to wealthy patrons, to eat butter and milk during Lent.

Fasting and feasting are a manifestation of the reality of the unity of the Mystical Body of Christ.

For now, though, we can say that fasting, like feasting, in Christian (and Jewish) tradition has always been "public and communitarian."[9] First of all, this is simply a manifestation of the reality of the unity of the Mystical Body of Christ. In the Mass, we worship together not only by being physically present in the same building but by standing, sitting, kneeling, and speaking in unison. In the same way, we mourn and celebrate together as the family of God.

But fasting together also serves an important physical role, in addition to the spiritual: It makes stricter disciplines more feasible for more people. First, we suffer and struggle together through the pangs of hunger, just as we suffer and struggle together through spiritual warfare and the constant onslaught of the evil one. In so doing, we strengthen one another with words of encouragement and, more so, with our example of perseverance.

---

9 Tessore, *Fasting*, 27.

At least as importantly, however, shared liturgical fasting (and feasting) is a culture-building force. To this day, in parts of the country with significant Catholic heritage, major fast-food chains promote fish sandwiches during Lent. This is a vestige of a real, living Catholic culture, one that transforms spiritual truths into embodied realities.

It is one thing to proclaim the words "For our sake He was crucified under Pontius Pilate; He suffered death and was buried, and rose again on the third day in accordance with the Scriptures." The genius of the Church has always been to make that claim tangible in the way we live, setting aside the days of Christ's death and of His Resurrection as undeniably special by forming the habits of the faithful on those days. And so, even in a society that has forgotten all about Christ, there is still a vague understanding, mediated through diner fish specials, that Friday is somehow *different*.

As we think about rediscovering the beauty and joy of fasting, this is something we must keep in view: While fasting is undeniably spiritually beneficial to the individual, fasting *together* has special benefits for the Church and for our wider society. By taking fasting seriously, we demonstrate that what we claim to be true about Christ isn't just abstract, but that it is the foundation of our very lives.

Reasons to Fast

What is the point to be pale-faced through fasting if then you become livid with bitterness and envy? What is the point of not drinking wine, if then you become drunk with the poison of anger? What is the point of abstaining from meat, which was created to be eaten, whilst tearing your brothers limb from limb with malice and calumny?[10]

Ultimately, we should fast for the same reason we should do anything else: It is pleasing to the Lord. Our sacrifices, so long as they are made for and to Him, give Him glory by demonstrating that we organize our lives around the reality of the triune God, not the gods of pleasure and power and worldly satisfaction. And fasting, as we have seen, has been preeminent among the sacrifices practiced by Christians and enforced by the Church from the very beginning.

---

[10] Maximus of Turin, *Sermones*, 18, quoted in Tessore, *Fasting*, 58.

But fasting, like any good work, also has other benefits. As the best thinkers have realized since at least Aristotle, virtue is developed by forming good habits—and ditching bad habits. And many of our most engrained habits involve actions that are essential to life, especially eating and drinking. We get used to certain foods and beverages at certain times, and it can be very hard to imagine forming habits different from the ones we're accustomed to.

These habits, like any, can be good or bad, but in twenty-first-century America, at least, it's fair to say that there are a lot of not-so-great food and drink habits. Fasting, especially on a weekly basis and even very lightly, can be a way of forming good habits and weakening bad ones. Setting aside days for limiting our consumption to particular foods at particular times forces us to be thoughtful (and

prayerful) about what we eat. And thoughtfulness about something as basic as food is good training for thoughtfulness about other aspects of our lives. When we ask ourselves if our food and drink habits glorify God, we can be reminded to ask if our other habits glorify Him as well.

Fasting, therefore, can also train the will. There are few feelings more primal than the urge to eat when we are hungry. (There's a reason the Church uses "appetite" as a synonym for "desire.") Training ourselves to endure these impulses for the sake of a higher good—namely, God—teaches us to place them in their proper place—namely, under the control of our reason. This bears fruit in other aspects of our lives when our appetites try to take the reins, especially sexuality.

What are some bad reasons to fast? We hinted at them earlier, but they all involve fasting to achieve worldly goods rather than spiritual ones. "Fasting" in order to get an attractive figure for beach season isn't really fasting at all: It's dieting. The fact that fasting properly may have side benefits for our health demonstrates how the things God wants for us are good for us, body and soul. But losing weight is not a good primary reason to fast on Fridays; honoring the Lord by commemorating His Passion and death is.

Also, as St. Maximus the Confessor points out above, if we become miserable and cruel while eating less food, we aren't *really* fasting at all. True fasting involves a turning to God and away from our appetites, including the appetites for anger, envy, and so on. If fasting from food results in spiritual struggles elsewhere, we need to confront those struggles—and perhaps adjust our fasting from food so that it doesn't cause more harm than good, for ourselves and those around us.

After all, as we said at the very beginning, fasting should be joyful. When we deny ourselves worldly satisfactions for a higher, heavenly good, we make the reality of the Trinity manifest in our lives. Let us pray that this book, by providing inspiration for simple and beautiful meals for times of fasting, will inspire us to make fasting a regular part of our spiritual lives.

Fasting in Modern Practice

There is an unbroken tradition of fasting in the Church from the first century to the present day. Indeed, there are few Christian spiritual practices—the Lord's Prayer comes to mind as an example—that are attested earlier or more universally than fasting.

Therefore, we can say that fasting demonstrates the unity of the Body of Christ *through time* in a way few other disciplines do. When we fast, we are participating not just in a community of the here and now but in a community that transcends generations. The pangs of hunger that we offer to the Lord—in commemoration of His suffering, in reparation for our sins, in preparation for spiritual milestones—are the same pangs felt by Christians for the last two thousand years.

Now, there's no question that the Church's disciplines have evolved, and generally in one direction—that is, toward laxity. As we will see, this has not, in fact, been a consistent trend; the law of fasting has gone this way and that, both formally and informally, through the years. But we cannot deny that today's rules are much less complex and demanding than those of past centuries.

The reason for this is articulated in Pope St. Paul VI's 1966 apostolic constitution *Paenitemini*, which defines the law of fasting and abstinence for the universal Church to this day. The Holy Father writes:

Holy Mother Church, although it has always observed in a special way abstinence from meat and fasting, nevertheless wants to indicate in the traditional triad of "prayer—fasting—charity" the fundamental means of complying with the divine precepts of penitence. These means were the same throughout the centuries, but in our time there are special reasons whereby, according to the demands of various localities, it is necessary to inculcate some special form of penitence in preference to others.[11]

In other words, the Church desires to emphasize, first, the *internal* aspect of penitence and, second, the importance of prayer and almsgiving in addition to fasting as means of expressing and nurturing true penitence. He continues—and here is a very important part for us in the prosperous West:

Therefore, where economic well-being is greater, so much more will the witness of asceticism have to be given in order that the sons of the Church may not be involved in the spirit of the "world," and at the same time the witness of charity will have to be given to the brethren who suffer poverty and hunger beyond any barrier of nation or continent. On the other hand, in countries where the standard of living is lower, it will be more pleasing to God the Father and more useful to the members of the Body of Christ if Christians ... offer their suffering in prayer to the Lord in close union with the Cross of Christ.[12]

The Catholic Church is a universal Church, through time and place. That means that she is a worldwide Church and must be responsive to the needs of the faithful around the globe. Pope St. Paul VI's stated intent in de-emphasizing fasting was to lighten the yoke on those Catholics whose everyday life includes a kind of fasting and for whom intensified prayer may be a better and more realistic way of penance.

But look closely and you'll see that the Holy Father specifically recommends fasting for the well-off—which, in global terms, means just about everyone reading this book! The decline of fasting in wealthy nations has been spiritually disastrous, not to mention specifically counter to the wishes of the Church. And so, in this section, we will discuss the letter of the law in the Church today—but also ways of fruitfully going beyond the law while remaining true to Catholic tradition.

----

[11] Pope St. Paul VI, *Paenitemini* (February 17, 1966), chap. 3.

[12] *Paenitemini*, chap. 3.

The Law of Fasting

Tracing the history of fasting regulations in the Church is no easy task, in large part because these regulations were generally local or regional in nature. But there were some suggestions and rules that applied more broadly. The first-century *Didache* included some prescriptions for weekly fasting and for fasting before Baptisms; the fourth-century Council of Nicaea fixed a period of fasting before Easter; and the later fourth-century Synod of Laodicea defined a strictly limited diet for the Lenten fast.

From the early centuries of the Church, however, differences developed between the East and the West. The East, for instance, generally stuck to the

guidance of the *Didache*, with Wednesday and Friday fasts becoming customary. In the West, on the other hand, Friday and Saturday fasts were more common, to mark the day of Christ's death and His day in repose. "Should we be feasting when He is lying in the tomb?" asked St. Peter Damian.[13]

While generally a spirit of tolerance prevailed regarding different regions' fasting practices, there were attempts by popes and councils to excommunicate those who didn't follow a particular pattern. By the early Middle Ages, perhaps, in part, due to the unnecessary rancor, the Western Church had settled into somewhat more relaxed official practices, with Fridays and (generally) Saturdays set aside for one meal a day and abstinence reduced to a prohibition of flesh meat. This seems to have been a reasonably stable equilibrium for several centuries.

By the late Middle Ages and the early Renaissance, we begin to see the extensive use of ecclesial power to dispense people, groups, or entire regions from aspects of Lenten disciplines in return for favors to the Church. The "Butter Tower" of the Cathedral of Rouen may be the most infamous example of this, but it is not the only one. By 1741, Pope Benedict XIV had had enough:

> How could we not lament that the most sacred observance of the fast of Lent has been almost completely eliminated due to the excessive ease of dispensing, everywhere, indiscriminately, for trivial and non-urgent reasons, so as to cause the just grievances of those who follow the orthodox Religion?[14]

In this encyclical, the pope implored the bishops not to approve blanket dispensations without "grave necessity" or, in the case of an individual, without the testimony of multiple medical doctors. Eighteen years later, Pope Clement XIII followed up with *Appetente sacro*, which reaffirmed his predecessor's plea "to recall the discipline of the Lenten fast, now weakened by many corruptions, to its original observance.... It perhaps remains for you to eradicate with God's help anything pertaining to the old or new corruption for breaking the laws of the fast ... or the customs which shy away from the true power and nature of the fast."[15]

By the time of the writing of *The Catholic Encyclopedia* in the early twentieth century in the United States, the fruits of the efforts of Popes Benedict XIV and

---

[13] *De ieiunio sabbati* 5, quoted in Tessore, *Fasting*, 42.

[14] Pope Benedict XIV, *Non ambigimus* (May 30, 1741).

[15] Pope Clement XIII, *Appetente sacro* (December 20, 1759), nos. 1, 2.

Clement XIII could be seen: While the Saturday fast had faded into memory, a strong tradition of fasting and abstaining from meat throughout the year remained. This included all the non-Sunday days of Lent, Fridays in Advent, the Ember Days, and several vigils.[16]

As the Second Vatican Council came to order, however, those who remember this era report that, apart from the Friday abstinence that was so engrained in Catholic culture, a spirit of laxity had again come into the Church. Fasting and abstinence had become, once again, a question of what could be plausibly excused rather than what we could offer to the Lord. It was in this context that a new generation chose a new approach to regulating Catholic fasting.

Who? When? How Much?

The current laws of fasting and abstinence were laid out for the universal Church in 1966 by Pope St. Paul VI in his apostolic constitution *Paenitemini*. An apostolic constitution is the most serious form of papal lawmaking in the Church; the disciplines laid out in such documents become part of the *Code of Canon Law*, which governs the Church.

But we have to do more than simply read *Paenitemini* in order to describe the current rules of fasting. This is because the document leaves a good deal of space for the episcopal conferences—that is, national bishops' conferences—to define particular rules within their territories. And so, as it has always been, while fasting as a discipline remains a constant in the Church, the specific practices of that discipline vary from place to place.

There are some aspects of fasting, however, that the Church insists must be truly universal:

> The days of penitence to be observed under obligation throughout the Church are all Fridays and Ash Wednesday, that is to say the first days of "Grande Quaresima" (Great Lent), according to the diversity of the rites. Their substantial observance binds gravely.... Abstinence is to be observed on every Friday which does not fall on a day of obligation, while abstinence and fast is to be observed on Ash Wednesday ... and on Good Friday.[17]

---

[16] James David O'Neill, "Fast," *The Catholic Encyclopedia*, vol. 5 (New York: Robert Appleton Company, 1909), http://www.newadvent.org/cathen/05789c.htm.

[17] *Paenitemini*, chap. 3. "Great Lent" refers to the title for the pre-Easter penitential season in many of the Eastern Catholic churches.

You will notice that the law of the universal Church, contrary to popular belief, is that *every Friday*—not just the Fridays of Lent—is a penitential day that ought to be marked by abstinence from meat. But this is one of the areas concerning which Rome has given flexibility to bishops' conferences, which may "substitute abstinence and fast wholly or in part with other forms of penitence and especially works of charity and the exercises of piety."[18] This is what the United States bishops have done: Fridays remain penitential, but there is no single prescribed way of performing this penance.[19] In contrast, the bishops of England and Wales recently reinstated abstinence as the specific form penance must take.

People often wonder whether notable feasts override Friday penance during Lent or throughout the year. In *Paenitemini*, Pope St. Paul VI continued previous practice by exempting the faithful from Friday penance only on days of precept—that is, holy days of obligation. But the 1983 *Code of Canon Law* slightly extended the exception to include all solemnities. Therefore, some major feasts that are generally not holy days of obligation, such as the Annunciation (March 25) and the Nativity of St. John the Baptist (June 24), would not be days of abstinence when they fall on a Friday. Also, there can be local solemnities, such as the patronal feast of a diocese or a parish, that lift the obligation of abstinence for those under the jurisdiction of that local church.

Now what, exactly, does the Church mean by fasting? There is still a clear preference, even in 1966, for a single full midday meal with no other snacks or "collations," which is just a term for a heavy snack (or a very light meal, as the case may be). But, in continuity with the evolution of the discipline to the modern day, "taking some food in the morning or evening" is "not prohibit[ed]."[20] This is usually expressed, then, as a maximum of one meal and two collations per fasting day.

The range of ages who are bound to fast and abstain is rather limited compared with Christian tradition, but this also is meant to ensure that no one receives a yoke that is too burdensome: Abstinence begins at fourteen and goes until death; fasting runs from age twenty-one to age fifty-nine. But, of course, younger children and older adults are free to participate and would likely benefit spiritually from doing so, even if just in a small way, within the bounds of prudence.

---

[18] Pope St. Paul VI, *Paenitemini*, chap. 3.

[19] United States Conference of Catholic Bishops (USCCB), *Pastoral Statement on Penance and Abstinence* (November 18, 1966), 24.

[20] Pope St. Paul VI, *Paenitemini*, chap. 3.

Flesh Meat versus Fish Meat

So what's the story on abstinence from meat? Many people have heard the stories of the lobbying of Roman fishmongers for the Church to set aside a day of the week for their benefit. Although, as we have seen, it hasn't necessarily been beyond the Church to respond to such special pleading (especially in return for some goodies), that is not the history of prohibitions on "flesh meat," as it is called in Church tradition.

Most fundamentally, the tradition of abstinence from meat is founded in the ancient understanding that we must be thoughtful and intentional about what we consume. After all, man's living body is both inseparable from his soul and a temple of the Holy Spirit. The Church Fathers speak with one voice that gluttony, in oversatisfying our bodily desires and thereby increasing their intensity, is very bad for the body and the soul.

Meat was one of the ancient delicacies that received special attention because, in excess, it represented both luxury and a kind of heaviness that privileges the

body at the expense of the soul.[21] Although the Church rejected the necessity of a strict vegetarian diet from her early days, "the Christian ideal soon developed a vegetarian tendency."[22] St. Basil expresses unease at the idea of butchery to satisfy the stomach,[23] and St. Augustine writes that abstinence "purifies the soul, elevates the mind, subordinates the flesh to the spirit, begets a humble and contrite heart, scatters the clouds of concupiscence, extinguishes the fire of lust, and enkindles the true light of chastity."[24]

Later, St. Thomas Aquinas describes the effects of meat from the perspective of pre-modern dietary science. It's not exactly how today's dieticians would describe the effects of various foods on the body, but it's not exactly wrong, either. The Angelic Doctor writes that the meat of land-dwelling animals is most like man and therefore is most pleasurable to eat and provides a kind of vigor and substance that is translated into other base passions—most notably, lust.[25]

All the ancient penitential dietary laws of the Church fall under the umbrella of *xerophagia*, a Greek word that means "dry eating." This includes six foods forbidden for being from animals or particularly pleasing to the senses: flesh meat, fish meat, dairy, eggs, wine, and oil. While these restrictions are associated with the Christian East—and are still in force in many Catholic and Orthodox churches—the fourth-century Synod of Laodicea proposed a canon, which was accepted by the rest of the Church, that made *xerophagia* the law of the Church during Lent.[26]

As we have seen, these rules were gradually relaxed over time, often through numerous exceptions given to favored people or groups that eventually became customs in themselves. Today, the remnant of *xerophagia* in the Latin Church is abstinence from the meat of land-going animals—with a few local exceptions for borderline cases, such as alligator in the Archdiocese of New Orleans. But we can confidently say that the history of abstinence from meat is one of genuine Christian concern for the health of body and soul—not for the pocketbooks of the fishmongers.

---

[21] See St. Clement of Alexandria, *Paedogogus*, bk. 2, chap. 1.

[22] Tessore, *Fasting*, 88.

[23] See *De jejunio*, sermo 1, 8. See "Appendix 1: Basil's Sermons about Fasting," Bible.org, https://bible.org/seriespage/appendix-1-basil%E2%80%99s-sermons-about-fasting.

[24] James David O'Neill, "Abstinence," *The Catholic Encyclopedia*, vol. 1 (New York: Robert Appleton Company, 1907), http://www.newadvent.org/cathen/01067a.htm.

[25] *Summa theologiae*, II–II, Q. 146, art. 8.

[26] See Tessore, *Fasting*, 93–94; Council of Laodicea, can. 50.

Mining the Tradition

If a little fasting is good, is a lot better? Should we look to the strictest disciplines of the early Church as a corrective for the more lax practices of today? What principles should guide our fasting and dietary choices as Catholics in the twenty-first century?

First of all, there's a strong tradition in Catholic spirituality that it's not a good idea to go it alone, in terms of making decisions about our spiritual lives. In the Rule of St. Basil, for instance, the saintly bishop recommends that monks fast and abstain as their brothers do, rather than make up their own rules.[27]

Meanwhile, several Church Fathers counsel moderation in fasting in order to avoid weakening the body so that it cannot undertake physical and spiritual work. The fourth-century pilgrim Egeria praised a local Christian community for this approach to fasting:

> No one compels how much anyone ought to do, but everyone does what they are able; those who have done much are not praised, nor are those who have done less reproached.[28]

Does this mean that we should do only what the Church has required since 1966, and no more, in order to participate humbly in the life of the Church in a unified way? Not so fast. Even the documents of the 1960s strongly recommend that Catholics maintain traditional disciplines and continue to mark important days and seasons with fasting and abstinence. They just removed the penalty of mortal sin for failing to observe them. Here are selections from the United States bishops' document on penance from 1966:

> For all other weekdays of Lent, we strongly recommend participation in daily Mass and a self-imposed observance of fasting.

> We suggest that the devout will find greater Christian joy in the feasts of the liturgical calendar if they freely bind themselves, for their own motives and in their own spirit of piety, to prepare for each Church festival by a day of particular self-denial, penitential prayer and fasting.

---

[27] See *Regulae brevis tratatae*, 82–83; see also Tessore, *Fasting*, 75.

[28] *The Pilgrimage of Egeria*, trans. Anne McGowan and Paul F. Bradshaw (Collegeville, MN: Liturgical Press, 2018), 28, 4.

Friday should be in each week something of what Lent is in the entire year. For this reason we urge all to prepare for that weekly Easter that comes with each Sunday by freely making of every Friday a day of self-denial and mortification in prayerful remembrance of the passion of Jesus Christ.[29]

And so, far from being an act of pride or disobedience, mining the tradition of the Church for ways to perform penance through self-denial is precisely what the framers of current disciplines had in mind. Fasting throughout Lent; fasting or abstaining from meat on Fridays through the year; fasting on vigils and Ember Days: These remain beautiful and spiritually fruitful parts of our Catholic patrimony that we mustn't be ashamed or afraid of.

It is important to add that if you decide to take up a particularly challenging practice of fasting, you should do so under the guidance of an experienced spiritual director. There are still dangers, to both the body and the soul, in do-it-yourself fasting that we must be aware of. But there is safety in sticking with the disciplines that have sustained generations of Christians for two millennia. In taking up those disciplines in prayerful humility, we unify ourselves with the Church through time—our forebearers in faith who were strengthened physically and spiritually by devout fasting.

---

[29] USCCB, *Pastoral Statement on Penance and Abstinence*, 14, 17, 23.

Lent

When we think of fasting, we think of Lent. That's for good reason: The pre-Easter fast is one of the most ancient in the history of the Church. And over the centuries, the Lenten fast, in all the forms it has taken in different times and places, has come to be a defining feature of Christian civilization.

We can even see the cultural impact of Lent in our increasingly post-Christian civilization. The biggest parties of the year in regions with deep Catholics roots, such as New Orleans (Mardi Gras) and South America (Carnival), were originally pre-fasting blowouts. Now they're largely secular, decadent, and vulgar; coming generations will need to be taught that somehow these spectacles were once essential parts of the Church's liturgical-cultural calendar.

But enough complaining! Lent is meant to detach us from worldly concerns and return our focus to Christ. While it is meant to be a quiet and solemn season, it is ordered not to grumpiness but to joy. This is the paradox of Lent: We renew our attention to Jesus Christ, who should always and everywhere bring joy; but it is the Christ of the Passion who is before our eyes, whose suffering brings feelings of grief and shame. How does this work?

The answer is pretty simple: We know how the story ends. We know that suffering, sin, and death don't have the last word. We know that Christ's suffering, like ours, is ordered not just to a greater good but to the highest good of all: our eternal life with the triune God. In this age of salvation history, we can and must relive, in some small way, the Passion of our Lord; but we do so in full knowledge of His final victory.

This is why fasting is especially appropriate, and meaningful, in this season. Fasting involves a physical deprivation that puts us in mind of spiritual goods; the experience reproduces the paradox of Lent in everyday life. We are reminded, as we follow in prayer and liturgy the progress of Christ to the Cross, that this world was never supposed to be comfortable and that suffering is unavoidable. And at the same time, by choosing to accept this deprivation, we open ourselves to the spiritual realities that make our suffering meaningful.

Therefore, like Christians through the centuries, we can experience grief and joy, shame and hope, pain and gratitude all at once—and make sense of them all. When we fast, especially during Lent, we are united with the Body of Christ not just here and now but through the ages. Just as we share with the other members the same Body and Blood of Christ in the Eucharist, we share the ritual of fasting for His sake. Together, we have consecrated this season of the Church's year and will continue to do so until He comes again.

The Invention of Lent

The details of Lent were not handed down to the Church by the Lord, like the stone tablets to Moses. Rather, like so many of the beautiful traditions we participate in, Lent developed through the habits of the faithful and the decisions of holy men of the Church to formalize those habits.

The origins of Lent aren't very easy to track down. Probably the fact that we can be most sure of is that the Council of Nicaea in 325—the same council that formalized the Nicene Creed, used to this day—prescribed a forty-day fast in anticipation of the celebration of Easter. But this wasn't really the *invention* of Lent as much as its *formalization*. Its roots go deeper.[30]

From the very earliest days of the Church, as described in the *Didache*, there was a period of fasting before Baptism for everyone involved in the rite. Further, the prescribed date for (noninfant) Baptisms in the Western Church was fixed at the Easter Vigil. (The East was somewhat more complicated, with a secondary date on "Lazarus Saturday," the week before the Vigil.) Therefore, we can see this pre-Baptismal fast as a precursor of Lent, which still culminates on a day set aside for Baptisms and receptions into full communion.

---

[30] Most of the historical details in this section come from William J. Tighe, "The Making of Lent," *Touchstone* 22, no. 2 (March 2009).

But the clearest predecessor of Lent is something completely different. In the early days of the Church in Egypt, a tradition developed of commemorating the forty-day fast of Christ in the desert with a fast of the same duration. Because Jesus undertook this fast *after* His Baptism, this fast began the day after Epiphany, which, at the time, commemorated both the visit of the Magi and the Baptism of Jesus (which involved a revelation, or "epiphany," of the entire Trinity).

This is where the duration of Lent that was formalized at Nicaea comes from. And so we can see that, through this organic development, Lent really has three spiritual purposes, all of which support one another: preparation for Easter; preparation for Baptism; and commemoration of Christ's fast in the desert.

And what happened to that ancient Egyptian fast? Well, a forty-day fast *after* Epiphany will always collide with a forty-day fast *before* Easter, and you end up with a fast from January 7 through mid-spring. Now, that is a very long fast, especially given the stricter practices in the early Church. Rather than have this lengthy and rather confusing mixture of fasts, the Egyptian fast, apparently at the urging of St. Athanasius in the fourth century, was folded into Lent.

Lent through Time and Place

Lent was officially fixed at forty days of fasting before Easter by the Council of Nicaea in 325. But which forty days? And what kind of fasting? Early divides in the traditions of Lent, it turns out, persist to this day.

There's no question that, from the very beginning, the Christian East took to fasting more strictly than the West. The tradition of "dry eating," or *xerophagia*, for instance, which bans all meat, fish, dairy, eggs, oil, and wine, developed in the East, was defined by councils of bishops in the East[31] and is still in force in the East, even if followed to the letter by few.

In the West, these disciplines were taken up sporadically and, as we have seen, by the late Middle Ages were often used as opportunities to solicit donations or favors in return for dispensations. This doesn't mean that Lent was easy in the West, at least compared with today. The Black Fast was something of a Western counterpart to *xerophagia* that allowed oil and sometimes wine and was

---

[31] The fourth-century Council of Laodicea and the seventh-century Trullan Synod are among the councils that required this strict diet for fasting seasons.

recommended by Sts. Ambrose and Bernard, among others.[32] The prohibition of eggs, as an animal product, is the basis for the Easter egg tradition.

Further, fasting and abstinence were required in the Latin Church on every non-Sunday of Lent until 1966 and usually consisted of only one meal per day after either Nones (afternoon prayer around three o'clock) or Vespers (evening prayer around six o'clock). Morning and evening collations eventually developed as accommodations but were described as such. The list of prohibited items on days of abstinence was also relaxed over time, from the Black Fast down to just meat by the twentieth century.

The definition of the forty days of Lent also diverged between the East and the West, with the former being, again, somewhat stricter and more stable through time. Lent in the East begins after Vespers on the seventh Sunday pre-

---

[32] James David O'Neill, "The Black Fast," *The Catholic Encyclopedia,* vol. 2 (New York: Robert Appleton Company, 1907), http://www.newadvent.org/cathen/02590c.htm.

ceding Easter and ends one week *before* Good Friday—forty straight days, with some loosening of fasting rules on Sundays. The weekend of Lazarus Saturday and Palm Sunday is outside the fasting season, then Great and Holy Week traditionally entails an even stricter fast than that followed during Lent.[33]

The exact definition of Western Lent has gone through several variations, including six weeks of five days of fasting in Milan (Saturdays and Sundays excepted) and six weeks of six days (Sundays excepted) in Rome. This latter fast, amounting to thirty-six days, was described by Pope St. Gregory the Great as a tithe of one-tenth of the days of the year to the Lord.[34] But at some point, apparently in the seventh century and out of embarrassment for missing out on the prescribed forty days, an additional four days were tacked on, resulting in the invention of Ash Wednesday.

Prayers for the Fast

In addition to fasting, Lent is meant to be a time of increased intensity in our prayer lives. Naturally, through the years, the Church has developed traditions of Lenten prayer that directly address fasting, asking the Lord to bless our hunger by turning our hearts back to Him.

In the Byzantine Rite, for instance, the daily prayers for the Lenten season are found in a book called the *Triodion*, named for the three odes (tri-odes) that appear in Matins during this season. Lenten Vespers includes the following prayer:

> While fasting with the body,
> brothers and sisters,
> let us also fast in spirit.
> Let us loose every bond of iniquity;
> let us undo the knots of every contact made by violence;
> let us tear up all unjust agreements;
> let us give bread to the hungry
> and welcome to our house
> the poor who have no roof to cover them,
> that we may receive mercy from Christ our God.

---

[33] Tighe, "The Making of Lent."

[34] Herbert Thurston, "Lent," *The Catholic Encyclopedia*, vol. 9 (New York: Robert Appleton Company, 1910), http://www.newadvent.org/cathen/09152a.htm.

In this beautiful prayer, we can see the essential connection between deprivation of the body and repentance in the soul. If we undertake the former while ignoring the latter, our fasting is nothing more than dieting—and miserable dieting at that. This is the same spirit found in a prayer attributed to Pope St. Pius V:

> Look with favor, Lord,
> on your household.
> Grant that,
> though our flesh be humbled
> by abstinence from food,
> our souls, hungering after you,
> may be resplendent in your sight.

The hunger we feel in our stomachs should enhance the hunger in our hearts for the Lord. And if it does, He will bless us, making our souls radiant.

Unsurprisingly, we can find some of the finest examples of fasting prayers in the early centuries of the Church, the golden age of Christian fasting. For many centuries, Prudentius was one of the most popular poets of that era; unfortunately, in the modern era, he has fallen into relative obscurity. Among the many lengthy hymns he composed for various occasions, he wrote two specifically for fasting—one for before and one for after the fast. Here are the first three stanzas of the Hymn for Those Who Fast, which accentuate the role of fasting as a sacrifice that trains the will and mortifies our unruly desires:

> O Jesus, Light of Bethlehem,
> True Son of God, Incarnate Word;
> Thou offspring of a Virgin's womb,
> Be present at our frugal board;
> Accept our fast, our sacrifice,
> And smile upon us, gracious Lord.
>
> For by this holiest mystery
> The inward parts are cleansed from stain,
> And, taming all the unbridled lusts,
> Our sinful flesh we thus restrain,
> Lest gluttony and drunkenness
> Should choke the soul and cloud the brain.
>
> Hence appetite and luxury
> Are forced their empire to resign;

The wanton sport, the jest obscene,
The ignoble sway of sleep and wine,
And all the plagues of languid sense
Feel the strict bonds of discipline.

And, finally, in the Hymn after Fasting, we find a reference to the fasting practice of Prudentius's time—no food until the ninth hour—the time of Vespers, or around 3:00 p.m. The poet praises the Lord for the blessings He sends to us for so little in return:

Nine hours have run their course away,
The sun sped three parts of its race:
And what remains of the short day
Fadeth apace.

The holy fast hath reached its end;
Our table now Thou loadest, Lord:
With all Thy gifts true gladness send
To grace our board.

Such is our Master's gentle sway,
So kind the teaching in His school,
That all find rest who will obey
His easy rule.

Rediscovering Lent

Today, the Church requires two Lenten disciplines: abstinence from meat on Fridays and fasting—one meal and two collations, or snacks—on Ash Wednesday and Good Friday. We all know that it is a pious tradition also to give up something enjoyable for Lent. This seems to be most commonly another food (sweets) or drink (alcohol), but technology (smartphones, social media, etc.) is quickly rising as a popular Lenten deprivation.

It goes without saying that the modern practice is much less severe than Christian fasts over the centuries. Although there is great value in fasting in a manner consistent with our brothers and sisters in Christ, we might also consider the Church's current discipline to be a starting point—a floor rather than a ceiling for our own practices.

The point of fasting, after all, is to deprive ourselves enough *really to feel it*—enough, that is, to make us feel a little desperate, to make us rely on God for spiritual sustenance as we suffer just a little from lack of physical sustenance. Further, the Lenten fast should be training our wills to rein in our unruly desires. In this regard, it is like a physical workout: If we aren't pushing ourselves to test our limits (within the bounds of prudence), we aren't growing.

We might consider using that pious practice of giving up something for Lent to expand our fasting horizons. Maybe we could choose something we can't imagine living without. Maybe we could choose an extra day of the week—Wednesdays and Saturdays are traditional—to fast. Maybe we could work with friends or family members to organize a group fast, with shared prayer and accountability.

One benefit of the Church's less restrictive rules today is that we can undertake these more challenging disciplines without fear of sin: If we find our self-chosen rules unbearable (or too easy), we can adjust them on the fly. As with any supererogatory practice (that just means "beyond what is strictly necessary"), we should consult a spiritual director to ensure we aren't doing more harm than good to our bodies and souls.

For many Christians today and through the ages, Lent has been the favorite season of the year. The deprivation from food and drink, combined with prayer, can result in something like a spiritual high that builds over the course of the forty days. And we anticipate and enjoy the indulgent celebration of Easter all the more intensely when we've really felt the pinch during Lent.

In short, the time is right for a rediscovery of Lent. Perhaps, just as has happened throughout the history of the Church, the habits of the faithful will develop new traditions that will become disciplines of the universal Church in the decades and centuries to come.

Fasting through the Year

Today, Christian fasting is almost synonymous with the season of Lent. But, as we have seen, this has not been the understanding of the Body of Christ through history. For Christians through the ages, while Lent was the most notable fast of the year, fasting was a regular aspect of the spiritual life during all the year. The *Didache*, for instance, prescribes fasting two days a week and dedicating that fasting "for those who persecute you."

The basic insight here is that fasting, with the right intention and for the right reasons, is an essential part of the spiritual arsenal of the Christian. We don't need to practice self-denial only in anticipation of Easter. The goods that fasting accomplishes in us, through God's grace, are spiritually fruitful at all times: strengthening our will, restoring prayerfulness to our everyday decisions, turning our focus back to God.

And so we can choose to fast really at any time and for any intention—a day here for a sick friend's healing, a few days there for a family member's conversion, maybe once a week for a year for the spiritual healing of our nation. These are just a few examples: The beauty of fasting, like its counterparts of prayer and almsgiving, is that its spiritual uses are truly endless.

At the same time, over the centuries the Church developed traditions of fasting so that we have some shared times of fasting as the Body of Christ. Further, specific times of fasting relieve the faithful of having to develop our own personal traditions, helping us to avoid both laxness and excess. Specifically, the Church has sought to apply reason to the practice of fasting by attaching it to days and seasons and liturgies that will make it especially efficacious for us, for our neighbors, and for the entire Body of Christ.

None of the fasts described in this section are binding on pain of sin since 1966, when Pope St. Paul VI shifted the emphasis from prescribed fasts to voluntary ones—and to prayer and charity, which he and other Church leaders at the time felt were being crowded out by rote fasting disciplines. But all of these fasts have a wonderful history in the Church, and all can be fruitfully practiced by the faithful today—while, at the same time, we also practice prayer and charity for the renewal of our own souls and of the Church.

In fact, in an age like ours, when authenticity is in such short supply and is highly valued for that reason, there's a special appeal to taking up some or all of these fasts. They bring the spiritual realities we speak and pray about into

the visible world, and they demonstrate a commitment to organize our entire lives—not just our Sundays—around the life of the Church. And they bring us in touch with the drama of salvation history as commemorated in the Church's liturgies, forcing us to think about this drama not just during set-aside "religious" times but every time we think about munching a snack or sipping a drink.

And that, finally, is one of the most beautiful things about the Church's fasting traditions: Like liturgy and sacraments, they engage the *whole person*, body and soul, in an act of sacrifice and worship and fidelity. And they do so not just in church but throughout our day and our year.

Fruitful Friday Fasting

Friday should be in each week something of what Lent is in the entire year. For this reason we urge all to prepare for that weekly Easter that comes with each Sunday by freely making of every Friday a day of self-denial and mortification in prayerful remembrance of the passion of Jesus Christ.

These are the words of the United States Catholic bishops in their 1966 statement ending the requirement that Catholics abstain from meat on Fridays throughout the year. While the intention was to begin a new era of self-chosen Friday penances, the result was that most of the faithful heard that meatless Fridays were over, and that was that.

But as we can see, the words of the bishops' statement really do articulate the beauty and meaning of the old Friday fast: Every week, we commemorate the life of Christ in miniature. Every Friday is a little Lent, or perhaps a little Good Friday. Every Sunday is a little Easter. Every week has a dramatic narrative that we bring to life through prayer and liturgy, yes, but also through the most basic decisions we make every day: what to eat, what to drink.

Now, today we all know that the way the bishops chose to try to instill this sense of weekly spiritual drama in the faithful didn't quite work out. But that doesn't mean we can't pick it up! Throughout the history of the Church, bishops and popes often found themselves ratifying the organic traditions of the people much more than imposing traditions from the top down. In the same way that we can help our fellow Christians and the institutional Church to rediscover Lent, we can help them to rediscover the weekly little Lent of Fridays.

After all, this fast is one of the most ancient and consistent in Church history. Even while the East and West argued over whether Wednesday (the betrayal of Judas) or Saturday (Christ in the tomb) should be the second weekly fast day, from the very beginning everyone agreed that Friday should be marked by significant self-denial.

If we commemorate Fridays in this way, it is also a reminder to commemorate Sundays as well. Of course there's Mass, but "keeping the Lord's Day" has always been about more than just an hour in church: It's the entire day we're meant to set aside. That means avoiding unnecessary labor and commerce as much as possible. But it can also mean some intentional feasting—a big family meal, a nice bottle of wine, a sumptuous dessert! This is the counterpart to the Friday fast, and they build each other up: Friday increases the anticipation for Sunday, and exuberant Sunday completes the austerity of Friday.

Taken together, Friday and Sunday observances remind us that we are never apart from the drama of our Lord's life, death, and Resurrection. They define reality for us—the reality of sin, the reality of forgiveness, the reality of grace, the reality of Heaven. And we bring them alive by commemorating them throughout each day.

Advent and St. Martin's Lent

The roots of Advent are at least as complicated, but not as ancient, as those of Lent. This is, in part, because the feast of Christmas wasn't celebrated by the universal Church until the fourth century, and even then—and to this day—it is celebrated on different days in the West and the East (January 7). It is for this reason, in turn, that Advent has developed as a phenomenon of the Western Church.

In the same way that Lent resulted from the formalization, over time, of previous traditions among the faithful, Advent took form over several centuries in the early Middle Ages. Its origins are probably French, for it developed from a tradition surrounding a particularly French feast: St. Martin's Day, November 11. The time from this day until Christmas was set aside as "St. Martin's Lent" and involved fasting according to the rules of Lent on Mondays, Wednesdays, and Fridays.[35]

---

[35] Francis Mershman, "Advent," *The Catholic Encyclopedia*, vol. 1 (New York: Robert Appleton Company, 1907), http://www.newadvent.org/cathen/01165a.htm.

The origins of Advent likely developed from the French tradition surrounding St. Martin's Day known as "St. Martin's Lent," which involved fasting according to the rules of Lent on Mondays, Wednesdays, and Fridays.

St. Martin of Tours was, and remains, one of the most beloved saints in France. A courageous soldier, Martin famously cut his cloak in two in order to give half to a roadside beggar. After retiring from the soldier's life, he pursued religious life as a monk and hermit but became renowned for his wisdom and holiness. It is said that when the people acclaimed him bishop of Tours, he hid among farm animals—but the honking of a goose gave him away. Thus we have the tradition of eating goose on St. Martin's Day.

But this is a book about fasting, so enough of that! St. Martin's Day developed into the major harvest festival of the season, especially in France, and also marked the imminent arrival of winter. For this reason, it was natural as the beginning of a fasting season, with this "Lent" bookended by tremendous feasts.

While St. Martin's Lent endured in some places, around the seventh century we see the formalization of the modern four-Sunday Advent.[36] This Advent, as we can see from its roots in a kind of Lent, was not a festive time of tinsel and red-nosed reindeer and so on but a penitential season. Advent looks forward not just to the first coming of Christ at Bethlehem but to His second coming at the end of time. Therefore, it is a time when we remember *both* the perfect innocence of the Christ Child *and* the final judgment; we focus on preparing ourselves in the spirit of His innocence and for His just judgment.

Fasting and abstinence have been part of this preparation for many centuries, though the rules of this fast have never been as structured as those for Lent. We might consider giving up something enjoyable, as we do in Lent, or setting aside snacks, or trying the Monday-Wednesday-Friday fast of St. Martin's Lent. However we mark this season, our fast will make the feast of Christmas all the more enjoyable.

Oh, and we might also consider keeping the most festive decorations in storage until the evening of the twenty-fourth and keeping the house festive until at least Epiphany (January 6)—and maybe all the way to Candlemas (February 2), if you really like Christmas lights. Those weeks—not the secular shopping season from Thanksgiving to Christmas—are the real Christmas season.

Ember and Rogation Days

The passing of the seasons is one of the great joys of the year—at least for people like me, who live in parts of the world with all four seasons. Every year includes the story of life itself, with the birth of spring, the vibrancy of summer, the bittersweetness of fall, and the dark beauty of winter. Further, the fact that springtime rebirth always follows the death of winter reminds us both of the Resurrection of our Lord and the heavenly rebirth, and ultimately resurrection, promised to all of us.

And so the seasons, while, on the one hand, merely the result of the tilt and rotation and revolution of our planet, are also full of spiritual meaning. We might even say they are catechetical, one of the innumerable ways God has placed the stamp of His love on creation. It was only natural, then, that the Church would seek to sanctify the passing of the seasons through liturgy and other devotional practices. This is the motive behind the Ember Days.

---

[36] Mershman, "Advent."

The highlight of the Rogation Days was a lengthy procession through the fields and local farms, accompanied by chanting of the Litany of the Saints.

The purpose of their introduction, besides the general one intended by all prayer and fasting, was to thank God for the gifts of nature, to teach men to make use of them in moderation, and to assist the needy.[37]

The Ember Days were also a way to co-opt—or, in a sense, to baptize—pagan seasonal ceremonies that were popular in Rome. The Church, at her best, finds and elevates the good in the practices of the world around her: It was good for the Roman pagans to give thanks for the seasons but wrong of them to dedicate their celebrations to false gods. The Church could redirect the good impulse of supplication and thanksgiving to the correct, and only, Source of all good things.

---

[37] Francis Mershman, "Ember Days," *The Catholic Encyclopedia*, vol. 5 (New York: Robert Appleton Company, 1909), http://www.newadvent.org/cathen/05399b.htm.

The Ember Day fasts have roots at least in the third century but were given their final dates and extended to the entire Church by Pope Gregory VII in the eleventh century.[38] Those dates are the Wednesday, Friday, and Saturday (comprising all three of the traditional Christian fasting days) after the first Sunday of Lent, Pentecost, the feast of the Holy Cross (September 14), and the feast of St. Lucy (December 13).[39] Traditionally, priestly ordinations were held on Ember Saturdays.

Rogation Days have a similar seasonal agricultural motive but have a more regional history. Held in the springtime "to appease God's anger at man's transgressions, to ask protection in calamities, and to obtain a good and bountiful harvest," they were mostly a medieval English phenomenon and were never extended to the universal Church.[40]

Due to their English roots, however, the Rogation Days have a foothold in American Catholicism, and some priests and parishes have brought them back. The highlight of the celebration of the major Rogation Day is a lengthy procession, traditionally through the fields of the local farms, accompanied by a chanting of the Litany of the Saints. The major Rogation Day is April 25, and minor Rogation Days are the three days before the feast of the Ascension—a kind of extended Vigil as we beseech the still-bodily-present Christ to bless our upcoming year of labors.

The Rogation Day fasts were no longer obligatory by the early twentieth century, but we are always free to mark these penitential—and liturgically remarkable—days with acts of self-denial.

Vigils of Feasts

What comes to mind when you think of vigils in the Church today? There's the Easter Vigil Mass, perhaps the most beautiful (and longest) liturgy of the year. There's Christmas Eve, for which every family has its special traditions. And you might think of Halloween—All Hallows' Eve—before All Saints' Day, which has very much taken on a life of its own.

---

[38] Mershman, "Ember Days."

[39] This has given rise to a mnemonic device: Lenty, Penty, Crucy, Lucy.

[40] Francis Mershman, "Rogation Days," *The Catholic Encyclopedia*, vol. 13 (New York: Robert Appleton Company, 1912), http://www.newadvent.org/cathen/13110b.htm.

Interestingly, though, the excesses of Halloween actually point us toward the history of vigils. The first vigils of great feasts are attested in the first centuries of the Church:

> In the first ages, during the night before every feast, a vigil was kept. In the evening the faithful assembled in the place or church where the feast was to be celebrated and prepared themselves by prayers, readings from Holy Writ, and sometimes also by hearing a sermon. On such occasions, as on fast days in general, Mass also was celebrated in the evening, before the Vespers of the following day. Towards morning the people dispersed to the streets and houses near the church, to wait for the solemn services of the forenoon.[41]

Vigils soon fell out of favor with Church officials, however, because the time between the evening vigil services and the morning feast-day Mass soon became a popular time of raucous partying. This was especially popular among the people because the vigil had been a day of fasting, and so they were primed to eat and drink to their hearts' content. But all of this violated the spirit of fasts and feasts, and so vigils were (at least officially) canceled for several centuries.

When vigils returned during the Middle Ages, the evening and nighttime services were eliminated, and the day was marked primarily by a fast in preparation for the next day's celebration. By the early twentieth century, there were seventeen vigils recognized in the Church's calendar, though in the United States, only four included mandatory fasting: Christmas, Pentecost, the Assumption, and All Saints. (Yes, we fasted on Halloween.)

All of these fasts and most of these liturgical vigils were abolished in the 1960s, though, once again, we find the American bishops warmly recommending fasting to the faithful: "We suggest that the devout will find greater Christian joy in the feasts of the liturgical calendar if they freely bind themselves ... to prepare for each Church festival by a day of particular self-denial, penitential prayer and fasting."[42] And this only makes sense: While denying ourselves some sustenance will certainly make feasting more enjoyable (not to mention healthier), more importantly, it will help to focus us on the spiritual meaning of the coming celebration.

---

[41] Frederick Holweck, "Eve of a Feast," *The Catholic Encyclopedia*, vol. 5 (New York: Robert Appleton Company, 1909), http://www.newadvent.org/cathen/05647a.htm.

[42] USCCB, *Pastoral Statement on Penance and Abstinence*, 17.

Fasting on vigils serves to highlight the cultural and spiritual importance of Catholic feasts by increasing the contrast between the feast and everyday life. But it's also valuable in itself, providing liturgical opportunities throughout the year to dedicate fasts to particular intentions that are dear to us. In so doing, we live in continuity with the tradition of the Church and the People of God through the centuries and carry that tradition into the future.

The Black Fast

Hitherto we have fasted only until none [3 p.m.], whereas, now [during Lent] kings and princes, clergy and laity, rich and poor will fast until evening.

— ST. BERNARD

The Black Fast is the most rigorous form of fasting in the history of the Church. Not only does the Black Fast limit the content and quantity of food eaten, but also the time during which the penitent can eat. Here are the basic rules for the Black Fast:

- The penitent can eat only one meal per day.
- The penitent cannot eat flesh meat, eggs, butter, cheese, or milk nor drink wine.
- During Holy Week, the penitent can only eat bread, salt, and herbs and drink water.
- The penitent can eat their one meal only after sunset.

Fasting practices have evolved during the history of the Church, but those Catholics who wish to engage in the same timeless traditions of the Church as the early Christians might wish to practice the Black Fast. This fast is not encouraged for young children, the elderly, or anyone suffering from poor health.

Information on the Black Fast was adapted from The Catholic Encyclopedia *(O'Neill, James David, "The Black Fast." The Catholic Encyclopedia, Vol. 2. [New York: Robert Appleton Company, 1907], www.newadvent.org/cathen/02590c.htm.)*

TRADITIONAL FASTING SUBSTITUTION LIST

Butter/ghee
* Oil, such as sunflower, canola, sesame, coconut, olive, etc. (1:1).
* For baking: 1 cup pureed avocado replaces 1 cup of butter.

Buttermilk
* Add 1 tsp vinegar to any of the milk substitutes (1:1).

Cream
* Coconut cream (1:1).
* Silken tofu and soy milk; blend equal parts together (1:1).

Crème fraîche
* Soy cream cheese or extra firm silken tofu processed with either soy yogurt or soy sour cream (1:1).
* Strained non-dairy yogurt, preferably soy (1:1); empty yogurt into a sieve lined with cheesecloth set over a bowl. Allow to drain in the refrigerator overnight.

Eggs
* Hydrated flax meal or chia seeds (1:1); replace 1 egg by mixing 1 Tbsp ground flax meal or chia seeds with 3 Tbsp water and let sit for 15 minutes until it forms a gel-like substance.

* Aquafaba, a brine strained from beans, most commonly chickpeas (3:1, 2:1 for egg white); use 3 Tbsp aquafaba per egg or 2 Tbsp per egg white. This can even be whipped to make meringue.
* Applesauce 1/4 cup (1:1).
* Banana 1/2 ripe, mashed (1:1).
* Silken tofu 1/4 cup, pureed (1:1).

Milk
* Plain, unsweetened plant or nut milk, such as soy, almond, rice, or oat (1:1).

Parmesan
* Nutritional yeast (1:1).

Whipped cream
* Both of the substitutions for cream can also be whipped for whipped cream (1:1).

Yogurt
* Non-dairy yogurt, such as soy, almond, cashew, or coconut (1:1). If the recipe calls for Greek yogurt, simply choose a Greek-style non-dairy yogurt.

RECIPES FOR
TRADITIONAL FASTING

An index of recipes in this book that do not contain meat,
eggs, milk products, or alcohol. Recipes throughout are
marked with a symbol like the one in the upper corner.

Fasting . . . cuts down to the depths, venturing into the soul to kill sin.

—ST. BASIL

Breakfast

Mixed Fruit Salad

SERVES 4

Ingredients

2 bananas, sliced thin

3½ Tbsp (50 mL) orange juice

2 oranges, filleted

2 apples, chopped

2 kiwis, chopped

⅔ cup (100 g) mixed berries

1 cup (200 g) Greek yogurt

1 Tbsp honey

Pumpkin seeds

Sesame seeds

Preparation

Drizzle the banana slices with the orange juice.

Mix the fruit in a bowl and distribute into bowls. Mix the yogurt with the honey and use as a topping for the fruit. Sprinkle the pumpkin seeds and sesame seeds over the yogurt.

Note: You may omit the Greek yogurt in order to make this a Fast meal.

Energy Smoothie

SERVES 1

Ingredients

½ lb (220 g) mango, chopped

¼ cup (60 mL) orange juice

¼ cup (60 g) plain Greek yogurt

½ cup (120 mL) milk

5 ice cubes

Preparation

Puree all the ingredients in a blender.

Baked Muesli

SERVES 4

Ingredients

3⅓ cups (300 g) steel-cut oats

1 cup (250 mL) apple juice

3½ Tbsp (50 mL) water

½ cup (50 g) cranberries

2 apples, grated

1 heaping cup (230 g) plain Greek yogurt

1 apple, sliced

1 mango, diced

2 bananas, sliced

¼ cup (50 g) butter, diced

⅓ cup (60 g) raw cane sugar

Preparation

Mix the oats with the apple juice, water, and cranberries.

Add the grated apples and yogurt to the oat mixture and stir.

Preheat the oven to 425°F (220°C). Divide the muesli mixture among 4 ramekins, distribute the fruit over the muesli, distribute the butter pieces over the fruit, and sprinkle the sugar over the butter. Brown the muesli on the top rack for about 5 minutes.

And [Moses] was there with the Lord forty days and forty nights; he neither ate bread nor drank water. And he wrote upon the tables the words of the covenant, the ten commandments.
—EXODUS 34:28

Homemade Crunchy Muesli

SERVES 4

Ingredients

½ cup (50 g) steel-cut oats

2 heaping Tbsp (20 g) slivered almonds

2 heaping Tbsp (20 g) cashews, chopped

2 heaping Tbsp (20 g) pumpkin seeds

2 heaping Tbsp (20 g) sunflower seeds

2 tsp (10 mL) canola oil

3 tsp (15 mL) maple syrup

½ tsp ground cinnamon

1 egg white (substitute 2 Tbsp of aquafaba to make this a fasting meal*)

¼ cup (30 g) dried cranberries or raisins

Preparation

In a bowl, mix the oats, almonds, cashews, pumpkin seeds, sunflower seeds, canola oil, maple syrup, cinnamon, and egg white.

Preheat the oven to 375°F (190°C). Line a baking sheet with parchment paper. Place the mixture on the baking sheet and press it flat. Bake on the center rack for about 10 minutes. Let the mixture cool, crumble it, and mix in the cranberries or raisins.

Consume dry or serve with milk and berries of your choice.

*See the substitution list on **pg. v**.

"And he humbled you and let you hunger and fed you with manna, which you did not know, nor did your fathers know; that he might make you know that man does not live by bread alone, but that man lives by everything that proceeds out of the mouth of the Lord."

—DEUTERONOMY 8:3

Yogurt Bowl

SERVES 4

Ingredients

2½ cups (500 g) plain Greek yogurt

3½ Tbsp (50 mL) honey

2 cups (400 g) mixed fruit, chopped

Preparation

Mix the Greek yogurt with the honey. Fold the fruit pieces into the yogurt mixture. Divide the yogurt into bowls and garnish with homemade crunchy muesli if desired (see previous recipe).

Porridge with Honey and Berries

SERVES 4

Ingredients

2½ cups (600 mL) milk

¼ cup (60 g) honey

1 cup (150 g) rolled oats

1 tsp ground cinnamon

1¼ cups (250 g) mixed berries

Preparation

In a pot, bring the milk and honey to a boil. Add the oats, reduce the heat, and simmer gently for about 10 minutes. Season with cinnamon. Add the berries to the warm porridge.

Muffins with Dates

12 MUFFINS

Ingredients

½ cup (120 mL) milk

2½ tsp (25 g) yeast

2 cups (250 g) white flour

½ cup (50 g) ground almonds

¼ cup (50 g) raw cane sugar

¼ cup (60 g) butter, diced

⅔ cup (100 g) pitted Medjool dates, chopped

Preparation

In a pot, warm the milk slightly and dissolve the yeast in it. Mix the flour, almonds, and sugar in a bowl. Add the diced butter. Pour in the milk and knead everything into smooth, elastic dough. Cover the dough and let it rise at room temperature for about 45 minutes.

Preheat the oven to 350°F (180°C). Grease a 12-cup muffin pan or line it with paper cups. On a lightly floured surface, knead the dough again, folding in the dates. Divide the dough into 12 portions, shape them into balls, and place them in the muffin pan. Bake on the center rack for about 25 minutes, until golden brown.

An act is virtuous through being directed by reason to some virtuous good. Now this is consistent with fasting, because fasting is practiced for a threefold purpose. First, in order to bridle the lusts of the flesh. ... Secondly, we have recourse to fasting in order that the mind may arise more freely to the contemplation of heavenly things. ... Thirdly, in order to satisfy for sins.

— ST. THOMAS AQUINAS

Sweet Potato Hash Browns with Fried Egg

SERVES 4

Ingredients

Five sprigs (10 g) fresh lemon thyme leaves

2½ lb (1.2 kg) sweet potatoes, peeled and coarsely grated

Sea salt

Black pepper, freshly ground

2 Tbsp canola oil

8 eggs

Preparation

Preheat the oven to 450°F (240°C). Line a baking sheet with parchment paper. Mix the thyme leaves with the sweet potatoes. Season with sea salt and pepper. Spread the sweet potatoes evenly on the baking sheet. Bake on the center rack for about 15 minutes. Heat the canola oil in a nonstick frying pan and fry the eggs over medium heat. Season the fried eggs with sea salt and pepper to taste.

"And when you fast, do not look dismal, like the hypocrites, for they disfigure their faces that their fasting may be seen by men. Truly, I say to you, they have their reward. But when you fast, anoint your head and wash your face, that your fasting may not be seen by men but by your Father who is in secret; and your Father who sees in secret will reward you."

—MATTHEW 6:16–18

Omelet with Fresh Herbs

SERVES 4

Ingredients

6 eggs

1 egg yolk

3 Tbsp fresh herbs such as parsley, chives, basil, dill, or tarragon, chopped

½ cup (100 mL) cream

¼ cup (50 g) butter

Sea salt

Black pepper, freshly ground

Preparation

Mix the eggs and egg yolk well with a fork. Add the herbs and cream and beat until fluffy. Season with sea salt and pepper.

Melt half of the butter in a pan and pour in the egg mixture. Over low heat, carefully stir a little, and then let the omelet set slowly and evenly. Place a plate upside down on the pan and carefully tilt the omelet onto the plate. Melt the remaining butter in the pan. Then slide the omelet back into the pan with the browned side up. Allow to set for 2 minutes. Serve immediately.

"Thus says the Lord of hosts: The fast of the fourth month, and the fast of the fifth, and the fast of the seventh, and the fast of the tenth, shall be to the house of Judah seasons of joy and gladness, and cheerful feasts; therefore love truth and peace."

—ZECHARIAH 8:19

Egg White Omelet

SERVES 4

Ingredients

12 egg whites

Sea salt

Black pepper, freshly ground

Canola oil

½ cup (30 g) mixed fresh herbs, such as chervil, fennel, parsely, or chives, minced

4 tomatoes, sliced

2 Tbsp olive oil

1 Tbsp white balsamic vinegar or white wine vinegar

Preparation

Beat three egg whites and season with a pinch of sea salt and pepper. Heat some canola oil in a nonstick frying pan. Add the egg whites, let them set lightly, spread a quarter of the herbs over the eggs, and fold the omelet closed. Repeat with the remaining eggs and herbs. Preheat the oven to 350°F (180°C). Place the omelets on the top shelf of the oven for about 2 minutes. Remove the stems from the tomatoes and cut them into slices. Mix them with olive oil and balsamic vinegar, and season with sea salt and pepper. Serve tomatoes with the omelet.

Prayer, mercy and fasting: These three are one, and they give life to each other. Fasting is the soul of prayer; mercy is the lifeblood of fasting. Let no one try to separate them; they cannot be separated. If you have only one of them or not all together, you have nothing.

—ST. PETER CHRYSOLOGUS

Eggs au Gratin

SERVES 4

Ingredients

8 eggs

⅓ cup (30 g) grated parmesan cheese

¼ cup (50 mL) cream

½ cup loose (30 g) fresh chervil or parsley leaves, chopped

Butter for greasing

¼ cup (50 mL) olive oil

Sea salt

Black pepper, freshly ground

Preparation

Boil the eggs for about 8 minutes, rinse with cold water, and peel. Cut the eggs in half crosswise and carefully remove the yolks.

Preheat the oven to 350°F (180°C). Mash the egg yolks with a fork and mix with the parmesan and cream. Fill the egg halves with the mixture. Grease an ovenproof dish with butter and place the egg halves in it. If necessary, cut the bottom of the eggs straight so that they are stable. Sprinkle the eggs with the herbs, drizzle with the olive oil, and season with sea salt and pepper. Bake on the center rack for about 15 minutes, until golden brown.

"If my people who are called by my name humble themselves, and pray and seek my face, and turn from their wicked ways, then I will hear from heaven, and will forgive their sin and heal their land."

—2 CHRONICLES 7:14

He uses food in moderation and gives God thanks.

—ST. JEROME

Soup

Pot-au-Feu-Style Vegetable Stew with Sea Bass

SERVES 4

Ingredients

¼ cup olive oil

1 leek, cut into strips

1 carrot, cut into strips

1 fennel bulb, cut into strips

1 garlic clove, pressed

Scant ½ cup (100 mL) white wine (omit to make this a fast item)

1½ cups (400 mL) vegetable broth

Pinch (0.5 g) saffron threads

1 lb (500 g) skinless, boneless sea bass fillet, washed, patted dry, and cut into pieces

Sea salt

Cayenne pepper

Tabasco

Preparation

Heat the olive oil in a pot; sauté the vegetable strips with the garlic. Add the white wine, vegetable broth, and saffron threads. Cook over low heat for about 5 minutes.

Add the fish pieces to the vegetable broth and cook for about 4 minutes. Then season the pot-au-feu to taste with sea salt, cayenne pepper, and Tabasco.

"Fear not, Daniel, for from the first day that you set your mind to understand and humbled yourself before your God, your words have been heard, and I have come because of your words."

— DANIEL 10:12

Carrot Soup

SERVES 4

Ingredients

¼ cup (50 g) butter

14 oz (400 g) carrots, thinly sliced

2 shallots, minced

1 Tbsp raw cane sugar

3 cups (700 mL) vegetable broth

⅔ cup (150 mL) orange juice

2 oranges, filleted

Sea salt

Black pepper, freshly ground

Pink peppercorns

Preparation

Melt the butter over low heat in a pot; sauté the carrots and shallots. Sprinkle the raw cane sugar over the vegetables and let it caramelize slightly. Add the vegetable broth and the orange juice and simmer gently over medium heat for about 25 minutes.

In the meantime, divide the oranges among four soup plates. Puree the soup in a blender and pass through a fine sieve. Season with sea salt and pepper and pour into the plates with the orange fillets. Sprinkle with pink peppercorns.

"Is not this the fast that I choose: to loose the bonds of wickedness, to undo the thongs of the yoke, to let the oppressed go free, and to break every yoke? Is it not to share your bread with the hungry and bring the homeless poor into your house; when you see the naked, to cover him, and not to hide yourself from your own flesh? Then shall your light break forth like the dawn…"
—ISAIAH 58:6–8

Potato Soup

Ingredients

¼ cup (50 g) butter

1 onion, diced

1 garlic clove, diced

14 oz (400 g) starchy potatoes, peeled and diced

3¾ cups (900 mL) vegetable broth

¾ cup (150 mL) cream

2 Tbsp dried marjoram

Sea salt

Black pepper, freshly ground

Preparation

Melt the butter in a pot and sauté the onion and garlic until translucent. Add the potatoes and fry briefly. Add the vegetable broth and cream. Let the soup simmer over medium heat for about 30 minutes. Then puree the soup in a blender and add the dried marjoram. Simmer gently again for about 5 minutes. Season with sea salt and pepper to taste.

Count it all joy, my brethren, when you meet various trials, for you know that the testing of your faith produces steadfastness. And let steadfastness have its full effect, that you may be perfect and complete, lacking in nothing.

—JAMES 1:2–4

Cream of Corn Soup

SERVES 4

Ingredients

3 Tbsp olive oil

3 shallots, minced

2 cups (450 g) whole-kernel canned corn, drained

3¼ cups (750 mL) vegetable broth

Scant ¾ cup (200 mL) cream

Sea salt

Cayenne pepper

Chili oil

Preparation

Heat the olive oil in a pot; sauté the shallots and corn. Add the vegetable broth and cream and cook over low heat for about 20 minutes. Remove ⅓ cup of corn from the soup and set aside. Then puree the soup in a blender and pass through a sieve. Season with sea salt and cayenne pepper to taste. Add the corn kernels back to the soup and bring to a boil again briefly. Divide the soup among four bowls and drizzle with chili oil.

As to foods, one ought to have the greatest and most entire abstinence, because as the appetite is more ready to act inordinately, so temptation is more ready in making trial, on this head. And so abstinence in foods, to avoid disorder, can be kept in two ways, one by accustoming oneself to eat coarse foods; the other, if one takes delicate foods, by taking them in small quantity.

—ST. IGNATIUS OF LOYOLA

Red Beet Broth
with Curd Dumplings

SERVES 4

Ingredients

1 cup (50 g) chives, sliced into thin rings

½ cup (120 g) quark (may substitute ricotta plus 1 tsp of sour cream)

1 egg yolk

2 tsp (10 g) butter, melted

2 Tbsp white flour

Sea salt

Black pepper, freshly ground

1 large red beet, cooked

3½ cups (800 mL) vegetable broth

Preparation

Mix the chives, quark, egg yolk, butter, and flour and stir until smooth. Season the mixture with sea salt and pepper. Using two tablespoons, form dumplings out of the mixture and cook them in boiling salted water for about 10 minutes.

In the meantime, peel the beet and cut into slices; then cut the slices into thin strips. Bring the vegetable broth to a boil and add the beet strips. Divide the soup into bowls, lift the sour cream dumplings out of the salted water, let them drain a bit, and then add them to the hot soup.

And when they had appointed elders for them in every church, with prayer and fasting, they committed them to the Lord in whom they believed.
—ACTS 14:23

Cold Tomato Soup

SERVES 4

Ingredients

1 lb (500 g) tomatoes

1 cup (250 mL) tomato juice

¼ cup (50 mL) white balsamic vinegar or white wine vinegar

2 Tbsp tomato paste

Sea salt

Cayenne pepper

Raw cane sugar

Tabasco

1 cucumber

2 Tbsp (30 g) plain yogurt

4 tsp (20 g) crème fraîche

4 tsp (20 g) mayonnaise

Juice of ½ lemon

1 Tbsp dill, chopped

Preparation

Plunge the tomatoes into boiling water for about 30 seconds; then rinse with cold water. Skin and quarter the tomatoes and remove the cores. Puree the tomatoes with the tomato juice, balsamic vinegar, and tomato paste in a blender and pass through a sieve. Season the soup with sea salt, cayenne pepper, raw cane sugar, and Tabasco to taste and refrigerate until cold.

Using a peeler, cut the cucumber lengthwise into strips, except for the seeded part. Mix the cucumber strips with the yogurt, crème fraîche, and mayonnaise and season with sea salt, cayenne pepper, lemon juice, and dill. Divide the tomato soup into bowls and place some of the cucumber strips in the center of each bowl.

"The days will come, when the bridegroom is taken away from them, and then they will fast in those days."
—LUKE 5:35

The WISDOM of
HOLY MOTHER CHURCH

POPE ST. PAUL VI, *PAENITEMINI*, CHAP. 1.

In the Old Testament ... one goes without food or gives away his property (fasting is generally accompanied not only by prayer but also by alms) even after sins have been forgiven and independently of a request for graces. One fasts or applies physical discipline to "chastise one's own soul" (Leviticus 16:31), to "humble oneself in the sight of his own God" (Daniel 10:12), to "turn one's face toward Jehovah" (Daniel 9:3), to "dispose oneself to prayer" (Daniel 9:3), to "understand" more intimately the things which are divine (Daniel 10:12), or to prepare oneself for the encounter with God (Exodus 34:28). Penance therefore ... is a religious, personal act which has as its aim love and surrender to God: fasting for the sake of God, not for one's own self.

Christ, who always practiced in His life what He preached, before beginning His ministry spent forty days and forty nights in prayer and fasting and began His public mission with the joyful message: "The kingdom of God is at hand." To this He added the command: "Repent and believe in the Gospel" (Mark 1:15). These words constitute, in a way, a compendium of the whole Christian life.

Therefore, following the Master, every Christian must renounce himself, take up his own cross, and participate in the sufferings of Christ. Thus transformed into the image of Christ's death, he is made capable of meditating on the glory of the Resurrection. Furthermore, following the Master, he can no longer live for himself but must live for Him who loves him and gave Himself for him. He will also have to live for his brethren, completing "in his flesh that which is lacking in the sufferings of Christ ... for the benefit of his body, which is the church" (Col. 1:24).

Ginger Broth with Noodles

SERVES 4

Ingredients

2 lemongrass stalks

10 cups water

2 carrots, chopped

2 celery stalks, diced

3 whole cloves

1 Tbsp peppercorns

1 Tbsp sea salt

6 oz (160 g) rice noodles

3 Tbsp soy sauce

3 ½ Tbsp (50 g) fresh ginger (about one 3-inch piece), peeled and julienned

1 chili pepper, julienned

4 scallions, sliced diagonally into rings

Preparation

Crush the lemongrass with a wide knife blade and cut it into pieces. Add it to the pot along with the water, carrots, celery, cloves, peppercorns, and sea salt. Bring to a boil; then reduce the heat and simmer without lid for 1 hour. Pour the stock through a fine sieve into another pot, and cook until reduced to about 4 cups.

Add the noodles, soy sauce, ginger, chili pepper, and scallions to the broth and simmer gently for 5 minutes.

We must fast with our whole heart, that is to say, willingly, whole-heartedly, universally and entirely.

—ST. FRANCIS DE SALES

Fasting is a school of self-control.

–ST. AMBROSE

Salad

Layered Salad

SERVES 4

Salad Ingredients

1 head of lettuce, shredded

4 radishes, julienned

2 scallions, julienned

½ cucumber, julienned

2 carrots, peeled and finely grated

¼ celeriac, finely grated

2 red tomatoes, sliced thin

1 yellow tomato, sliced thin

1 avocado, sliced into a fan shape

Dressing Ingredients

¼ cup (50 g) plain yogurt

1 Tbsp mango vinegar or apple cider vinegar

2 Tbsp olive oil

Sea salt

Black pepper, freshly ground

Croutons Ingredients

2 tsp (10 g) butter

1 garlic clove, minced

2 slices of sandwich bread, cubed and crusts removed

Sea salt

Preparation

Layer the vegetables in a jar.

For the dressing, whisk the yogurt with the vinegar and olive oil and season with sea salt and pepper.

For the croutons, melt the butter in a pan, add the garlic and the bread cubes, season with a little sea salt, and fry until golden. Top the salad with the croutons.

"Yet even now," says the Lord, "return to me with all your heart, with fasting, with weeping, and with mourning; and rend your hearts and not your garments."
—JOEL 2:12–13

Wild Greens

SERVES 4

Ingredients

2 Tbsp (30 mL) raspberry vinegar or apple cider vinegar

3½ Tbsp (50 mL) canola oil

1 yellow bell pepper, diced

6 radishes, sliced thin

3½ Tbsp (50 mL) white vinegar

4 eggs, beaten

9 oz (250 g) mixed fresh wild greens, such as dandelion greens, frisée, and bibb lettuce, washed and dried

¾ cup (100 g) raspberries

Fresh herbs, such as edible flowers, parsley, or dill, for garnish

Preparation

Whisk the raspberry vinegar with the canola oil; add the bell pepper and radishes and mix. Season with sea salt and pepper. Dress the mixed fresh wild greens.

In a saucepan, bring water to a boil and add the white vinegar. Stir the water with the handle of a wooden spoon to create a swirl. Carefully slide the beaten eggs into it. Poach the eggs over low heat for about 5 minutes. Carefully lift out the eggs with a skimmer, place on the salad, and salt lightly. Sprinkle the raspberries and fresh herbs on top.

The soul who wishes to rise above imperfection should . . . remain fasting and watching, the eye of her intellect fastened on the doctrine of My Truth, and she will become humble because she will know herself in humble and continual prayer and holy and true desire.
—ST. CATHERINE OF SIENA

Fennel and Onion Salad

SERVES 4

Ingredients

2 fennel bulbs, julienned

12 oz (300 g) carrots, julienned

6 radishes, sliced thin

1 onion, cut into thin rings

1 oz (30 g) pitted black olives, halved

1 oz (30 g) pitted green olives, halved

1 lemon

1 tsp white balsamic vinegar or white wine vinegar

1 tsp maple syrup

⅓ cup (70 mL) olive oil

Sea salt

Black pepper, freshly ground

Preparation

Mix the fennel, carrots, radishes, onion, and olives in a bowl. Wash the lemon and finely grate half of the zest. Squeeze the juice into a small bowl and add the balsamic vinegar, maple syrup, and lemon zest. Gradually whisk in the olive oil and season with sea salt and pepper. Toss the dressing with the salad.

"Is not this the fast that I choose: to loose the bonds of wickedness, to undo the thongs of the yoke, to let the oppressed go free, and to break every yoke?"
—ISAIAH 58:6

Zucchini and Orange Salad

SERVES 4

Ingredients

2 blood oranges or orange of choice

2 zucchini, sliced thin

3 scallions, sliced diagonally into thin rings

2 Tbsp mango vinegar or rice wine vinegar

3 Tbsp olive oil

Sea salt

Black pepper, freshly ground

Preparation

Fillet one orange and squeeze the juice out of the other. In a bowl, combine the zucchini, orange fillets, and scallions. In a small bowl, whisk the orange juice with the vinegar and olive oil. Season the dressing with sea salt and pepper. Toss the dressing into the salad.

The scripture is full of places that prove fasting to be not the invention of man but the institution of God, and to have many more profits than one. And that the fasting of one man may do good unto another, our Saviour showeth himself where he saith that some kind of devils cannot be cast out of one man by another "without prayer and fasting."

—ST. THOMAS MORE

Arugula Lentil Salad

SERVES 4

Ingredients

½ cup (100 g) red lentils

8 oz (200 g) arugula

1 red onion, cut into thin rings

1 pear, sliced thin

½ cup (100 g) plain yogurt

2 Tbsp olive oil

1 Tbsp passion-fruit vinegar or rice wine vinegar

Sea salt

Black pepper, freshly ground

Preparation

Bring a pot of water to a boil, add the lentils, and cook for about 10 minutes. Drain the lentils, salt them a little, and let them cool. Mix the arugula, lentils, onion, and pear and arrange on plates. Whisk the yogurt with the olive oil and vinegar and season with sea salt and pepper. Drizzle the dressing over the salad.

"Go, gather all the Jews to be found in Susa, and hold a fast on my behalf, and neither eat nor drink for three days, night or day. I and my maids will also fast as you do. Then I will go to the king, though it is against the law; and if I perish, I perish."
—ESTHER 4:16

Eggplant Salad

SERVES 4

Ingredients

⅓ cup olive oil

2 eggplants, stem removed and sliced ¼ inch (1 cm) thick

Sea salt

Black pepper, freshly ground

1 tsp Ras el hanout or ground coriander

12 stalks asparagus, trimmed

2 Tbsp lemon olive oil*

1 Tbsp lemon juice

2 Tbsp (30 g) cedar or pine nuts

½ cup (100 g) cherry tomatoes, halved

½ cup (30 g) fresh mint leaves

½ cup (30 g) Italian parsley leaves

⅓ cup (50 g) pomegranate seeds

Preparation

Heat the olive oil in a nonstick frying pan and fry the eggplant slices over medium heat until light brown on both sides. Season with sea salt and pepper and drain on paper towels. Coarsely dice the eggplant and season with the ras el hanout.

Blanch the asparagus by submerging into salted boiling water for no more than 2 minutes, then removing and transferring to an ice water bath.

Whisk the lemon olive oil with the lemon juice and season with sea salt and pepper. Toast the cedar nuts in a pan without fat over medium heat until they smell fragrant and begin to brown, then remove from heat. Arrange the eggplant and the asparagus on plates, spread the tomatoes and herbs on top, and drizzle with the dressing. Sprinkle the salad with the pomegranate seeds and the cedar nuts.

If you cannot find lemon olive oil, you can make your own by warming (do not allow it to bubble) lemon peels in olive oil for 15 minutes, allowing the oil to cool, then straining the peels from the oil.

I sat down and wept, and mourned for days; and I continued fasting and praying before the God of heaven. …"O Lord, let your ear be attentive to the prayer of thy servant, and to the prayer of thy servants who delight to fear thy name…"

—NEHEMIAH 1:4, 11

Bread Salad

SERVES 4

Salad Ingredients

8 oz (200 g) ciabatta, cubed

Olive oil for frying

2 garlic cloves, thinly sliced

1¾ lb (700 g) pink beefsteak tomatoes, cubed

1 red onion, thinly sliced

4 oz (100 g) arugula

4 sprigs (¾ oz, 20 g) fresh basil

¼ cup (50 g) pitted black olives

Dressing Ingredients

Juice of ½ lemon

2 Tbsp balsamic vinegar

Sea salt

Black pepper, freshly ground

Preparation

For the dressing, whisk the lemon juice with the balsamic vinegar and season with sea salt and pepper.

For the salad, preheat the oven to 425°F (220°C). Place the bread cubes on a baking sheet and toast on the center rack for 5 minutes.

Heat a little olive oil in a pan; add the garlic and bread bites and sauté briefly. Season with sea salt and pepper. Remove the bread bites and garlic from the pan. In a bowl, mix the tomatoes, onion, arugula, basil, olives, and bread bites and toss in the salad dressing.

[Jesus] was in the wilderness forty days, tempted by Satan; and he was with the wild beasts; and the angels ministered to him.
—MARK 1:13

Penance also demands that we satisfy divine justice by fasting.

–POPE CLEMENT XIII

Collations

Marinated Asparagus with Avocado

Ingredients

2 lbs green asparagus

2 Tbsp lemon olive oil*

2 Tbsp vegetable stock

1 clove of garlic

1 Tbsp white balsamic vinegar or white wine vinegar

Sea salt

Black pepper, freshly ground

1 avocado

¾ cup feta cheese

3 tsp fresh basil leaves, washed and dried

Preparation

Trim the ends of the asparagus. Heat a tablespoon of lemon olive oil and sauté the asparagus. Deglaze with vegetable stock and steam, covered, for about 5 minutes, until firm to the bite. Peel and finely chop the garlic, add to the asparagus, and remove the pan from the heat. Add the balsamic vinegar and the remaining lemon olive oil and season with sea salt and pepper. Let the asparagus marinate for 30 minutes.

Peel the avocado, remove the stone, and slice the avocado thinly into a fan shape. Carefully arrange the asparagus with the avocado slices. Cut the feta into small cubes and spread over the vegetables. Garnish the dish with basil.

If you cannot find lemon olive oil, you can make your own by warming (do not allow it to bubble) lemon peels in olive oil for 15 minutes, allowing the oil to cool, then straining the peels from the oil.

"For the Lord your God is gracious and merciful and will not turn away his face from you, if you return to him."
—2 CHRONICLES 30:9

Potato Pancakes

SERVES 4

Pancake Ingredients

2¼ lb (1 kg) starchy potatoes, boiled, cooled, peeled, and grated finely

Zest of 1 lemon

¾ cup (150 g) semolina flour

1 cup (200 g) sour cream

2 eggs

¼ cup (50 g) raw cane sugar

1 tsp ground cinnamon

Butter for frying

Plum Sauce Ingredients

Scant ½ cup (100 ml) red wine

1 cinnamon stick

2 cloves

¼ cup (50 g) raw cane sugar

1 lb (500 g) plums, pitted and halved

Pancake Preparation

Preheat the oven to 220°F (100°C). Add the lemon zest to the grated potatoes. Mix the semolina, sour cream, eggs, raw cane sugar, and cinnamon. Add the mixture to the potatoes, mix well, cover, and let soak for about 30 minutes.

Heat some butter in a nonstick frying pan. Cut the potato dough into quarters and spread one quarter evenly in the pan. Over medium heat, cook the potato dough for 10 minutes, or until the underside is lightly browned. Flip the pancake and cook for another 5 minutes. Repeat for the rest of the dough. Keep the finished potato pancakes warm in the oven.

Plum sauce (*optional*)

Heat the red wine with the cinnamon stick, cloves, and cane sugar in a pot. Add the plums and cook over low heat until soft, about 15 minutes. Serve over the potato pancake.

The more one mortifies his natural inclinations, the more he renders himself capable of receiving divine inspirations and of progressing in virtue.

—ST. FRANCIS DE SALES

Quesadillas with Spinach and Ricotta

SERVES 4

Tortilla Ingredients

1 ½ cups (250 g) white flour

1 tsp sea salt

1 tsp baking powder

¼ cup (50 mL) butter, melted

¾ cup (150 mL) water

Filling Ingredients

3 ½ oz (100 g) spinach, blanched in salted water and squeezed dry

½ cup (120 g) ricotta

3 Tbsp (25 g) fresh basil, minced

½ cup (40 g) parmesan cheese, grated

1 Tbsp lemon olive oil*

Sea salt

Black pepper, freshly ground

Preparation

Mix the flour, sea salt, and baking powder in a bowl. Add the butter and water and knead into elastic dough. Let the dough rest for about 30 minutes.

Divide the dough into 8 portions. Place the dough between 2 sheets of plastic wrap and flatten it into tortillas about ⅛ inch (3 mm) thick. Cook on both sides over medium heat in a nonstick pan without grease.

For the filling, mix the spinach, ricotta, basil, parmesan, and lemon olive oil. Season with sea salt and pepper. Divide the mixture among 4 tortillas and place the remaining tortillas on top.

If you cannot find lemon olive oil, you can make your own by warming (do not allow it to bubble) lemon peels in olive oil for 15 minutes, allowing the oil to cool, then straining the peels from the oil.

"I have not come to call the righteous, but sinners to repentance."
—LUKE 5:32

Caponata with Burrata

SERVES 4

Ingredients

⅓ cup (50 g) pine nuts

4 or 5 roma tomatoes

4 Tbsp olive oil

½ cup (100 g) shallots, diced

1 tsp raw cane sugar

1 Tbsp white balsamic vinegar or white wine vinegar

1 large (200 g) eggplant, diced

2 sticks (100 g) celery, diced

½ large (100 g) red bell pepper, diced

½ large (100 g) yellow bell pepper, diced

¼ cup (50 g) capers

Sea salt

Black pepper, freshly ground

4 burrata cheeses

Lemon olive oil*

Preparation

Roast the pine nuts in a pan without fat. Blanch the tomatoes briefly and immediately rinse with cold water. Peel the tomatoes, cut them into quarters, and remove the core. Cut the tomatoes into small cubes.

Sauté the shallots in 1 or 2 tablespoons of olive oil. Add the diced tomatoes, sprinkle with the sugar, deglaze with the balsamic vinegar, and set aside.

In another pan, sauté the rest of the vegetables in the remaining olive oil. Add the shallot-tomato mixture, the capers, and the pine nuts and season with sea salt and pepper. Arrange the lukewarm vegetables on plates. Place one burrata on each, sprinkle with a little sea salt, and drizzle with lemon olive oil.

If you cannot find lemon olive oil, you can make your own by warming (do not allow it to bubble) lemon peels in olive oil for 15 minutes, allowing the oil to cool, then straining the peels from the oil.

"Wash yourselves; make yourselves clean; remove the evil of your doings from before my eyes; cease to do evil, learn to do good; seek justice, correct oppression; defend the fatherless, plead for the widow."
—ISAIAH 1:16–17

Fried Tofu

SERVES 4

Ingredients

20 oz (800 g) natural tofu, cut into long strips

Sea salt

Black pepper, freshly ground

2 Tbsp sesame oil

3 garlic cloves, sliced thin

2 Tbsp (20 g) candied ginger, chopped (optional)

2 red chili peppers, minced

¾ cup (200 mL) vegetable broth

½ cup (120 mL) soy sauce

3 bok choy, quartered and blanched

Preparation

Season the tofu with sea salt and pepper.

In a pan, heat the sesame oil and sear the tofu on all sides; set it aside.

In a sauté pan, heat the garlic, ginger, chili peppers, vegetable broth, and soy sauce. Add the bok choy. Cook until the liquid is syrup-like.

Arrange the bok choy on a plate and drip the soy reduction over it. Arrange the tofu over the bok choy.

He who wishes to find Jesus should seek Him, not in the delights and pleasures of the world, but in mortification of the senses.
—ST. ALPHONSUS LIGUORI

Marinated Artichokes with Pine Nut Cream

SERVES 4

Ingredients

4 large artichokes

½ lemon

6 oz (175 g) pine nuts

½ cup (100 g) mascarpone

3 Tbsp (10 g) fresh chervil leaves

Sea salt

Black pepper, freshly ground

2 limes

4 Tbsp olive oil

Scant ½ cup (100 mL) cream

2 tomatoes, blanched, diced, and lightly salted

Preparation

In a pot, bring salted water to a boil. Carefully break off the stems from the artichokes. Using kitchen shears, cut off the pointy leaf tips. Put the artichokes and lemon half into the boiling water and lower heat to simmer. Simmer until the leaves can be pulled out easily (about 35 min.). Remove the artichokes and let them drip dry.

In a pan without oil, roast the pine nuts until light brown. Set aside one tablespoon of pine nuts for garnish. Puree the remaining pine nuts, the mascarpone, and the chervil leaves in a blender. Season the mixture with sea salt and pepper.

Mix the juice of one lime with the olive oil and season with sea salt and pepper to taste.

Carefully pull out the artichoke leaves. With a spoon, remove the choke from the artichoke bottoms. Place the artichokes on a plate and drizzle them with a little of the olive oil marinade. Save the rest of the marinade.

Fillet the other lime. Whip the cream until stiff and stir it into the pine nut mix. Fill the cavity of the artichoke bottoms with the pine nut cream, spread the remaining olive oil marinade on top, and garnish with the remaining pine nuts, diced tomatoes, artichoke leaves, and lime slices.

Eggs au Gratin with Vegetables

SERVES 4

Ingredients

2 tsp fennel seed

Sea salt

3 Tbsp (40 mL) lemon olive oil*

7 scallions, sliced into ¼-inch rings

2 red bell peppers, julienned

2 yellow bell peppers, julienned

1 chili pepper, minced

2 garlic cloves, minced

Black pepper, freshly ground

2 avocados, chopped

1 cup (200 g) feta

8 eggs

Preparation

Crush the fennel seed in a mortar and mix with a little sea salt. Heat the lemon olive oil in a frying pan; sauté the scallions and bell peppers until slightly softened. Add the chili pepper and garlic and sauté briefly. Season the mixture with the fennel and salt mixture and pepper.

Preheat the oven to 400°F (200°C). Divide the vegetables among 4 small, ovenproof dishes. Place the avocado pieces on top, roughly crush the feta with a fork, and spread it on top as well. Crack 2 eggs into each of the dishes. Bake on the bottom rack for about 15 minutes.

If you cannot find lemon olive oil, you can make your own by warming (do not allow it to bubble) lemon peels in olive oil for 15 minutes, allowing the oil to cool, then straining the peels from the oil.

"…Return to the Lord your God, you and your children, and obey his voice in all that I command you this day, with all your heart and with all your soul."
—DEUTERONOMY 30:2

Roasted Vegetables with Herb Dip

SERVES 4

Vegetables

16 baby carrots, peeled

4 spring leeks, halved

6 baby red beets, halved

12 new potatoes

¼ cup (50 mL) olive oil

Sea salt

2 tsp (10 g) fresh rosemary leaves

Dip Ingredients

¾ cup (180 g) crème fraîche

1¼ cups (250 g) Greek yogurt

⅓ cup (25 g) mixed fresh herbs (e.g., chervil, chives, parsley), minced

Sea salt

Black pepper, freshly ground

Preparation

Preheat the oven to 400°F (200°C). Line a baking sheet with parchment paper.

Mix the vegetables with the olive oil, salt slightly, place on the baking sheet, and sprinkle with the rosemary. Roast on the center rack for 20 minutes, or until the vegetables are soft.

For the dip, mix the crème fraîche with the Greek yogurt and the herbs and season with sea salt and pepper to taste.

"Strive to enter by the narrow door; for many, I tell you, will seek to enter and will not be able."

—LUKE 13:24

Baked Semolina

Ingredients

2 abundant cups (500 mL) milk

Sea salt

Black pepper, freshly ground

Pinch of nutmeg, freshly grated

¾ cup (130 g) semolina flour

3 eggs

Butter for greasing

¼ cup (60 g) butter, melted

1 cup (100 g) grated parmesan cheese

Preparation

Bring the milk to a boil and season with sea salt, pepper, and nutmeg. Add the semolina and simmer for about 15 minutes, stirring occasionally. Remove from the heat and allow to cool briefly. Beat the eggs and fold into the mixture.

Preheat the oven to 400°F (200°C). Butter a gratin dish, pour in the semolina mixture, and smooth it down. Pour melted butter over the semolina. Sprinkle the parmesan on top and bake on the center rack for about 30 minutes, until golden.

Fasting cleanses the soul, raises the mind, subjects one's flesh to the spirit, renders the heart contrite and humble, scatters the clouds of concupiscence, quenches the fire of lust, and kindles the true light of chastity. Enter again into yourself.

—ST. AUGUSTINE OF HIPPO

Zucchini Hash Browns with Avocado Cottage Cheese and Smoked Salmon

SERVES 4

Ingredients

1¼ lb (600 g) zucchini, coarsely grated

1 lb (500 g) carrots, coarsely grated

Sea salt

1 lemon

1 ripe avocado, diced

1½ cups (300 g) cottage cheese

Black pepper, freshly ground

⅓ cup (25 g) chives, sliced into fine rings

5 Tbsp olive oil

2 shallots, diced

2 eggs, beaten

¼ cup (20 g) quick oats

⅓ cup (25 g) watercress

10 oz (300 g) smoked salmon

Preparation

Mix the grated zucchini and carrots with a little sea salt and set aside for about 20 minutes. Meanwhile, wash and dry the lemon, finely grate the zest, and squeeze two tablespoons of lemon juice. Toss the avocado with the lemon juice. Mix in the cottage cheese and lemon zest and season with sea salt and pepper. Add the chives.

Heat 1 tablespoon of olive oil; sauté the shallots until translucent. Transfer the shallots to a bowl. Place the zucchini and carrots on paper towels and squeeze vigorously. Then add the zucchini and carrots to the shallots and mix well. Mix in the eggs and the oats and season with sea salt and pepper. Form small, even-sized piles of the hash mixture, flatten them, and fry them in the remaining olive oil until crispy on both sides. Drain the fried hash browns briefly on paper towels. Then arrange the hash browns on plates, add the avocado cottage cheese, and sprinkle with watercress. Garnish with the salmon.

Bread Pudding
Carthusian Style

SERVES 4

Ingredients

½ cup (90g) raisins

3 Tbsp (40 mL) apple juice

15 slices of toast, buttered and cut in half

5 tsp (30 g) butter

3 eggs

1¼ cups (300 mL) milk

1¼ cups (300 mL) cream

½ cup (100 g) raw cane sugar

2 Tbsp (10 g) vanilla sugar or vanilla extract

1 Tbsp ground cinnamon

Preparation

Soak the raisins in the apple juice overnight.

Preheat the oven to 350°F (180°C). Place the slices of toast in a greased gratin pan in a brick-like pattern and sprinkle the raisins over them.

Stir together the eggs, milk, cream, half of the cane sugar, the vanilla sugar (or vanilla extract), and the cinnamon and pour the mixture over the bread. Sprinkle the remaining cane sugar on top and cover the pan with aluminum foil. Bake on the center rack for about 20 minutes. Remove the aluminum foil and bake for an additional 20 minutes, until golden brown.

I rent my garments and my mantle, and pulled hair from my head and beard, and sat appalled. ... And at the evening sacrifice I rose from my fasting, with my garments and my mantle rent, and fell upon my knees and spread out my hands to the Lord my God...

—EZRA 9:3, 5

Rice Pudding Benji Style

SERVES 4

Ingredients

1 vanilla pod or 1 tsp of vanilla paste or extract

4 cups (1 L) milk

1 cup (250 g) uncooked white rice, rinsed

1 cup (200 g) raw cane sugar

Zest of 1 lemon

Scant ½ cup (100 mL) apple juice

4 Boskop* apples, peeled and diced

1 tsp ground cinnamon

1 tsp ground tonka bean (or ½ tsp almond extract)

Honey

Preparation

Cut the vanilla pod in half lengthwise and scrape out the pulp. Bring the milk to a boil in a saucepan. Add the uncooked rice, vanilla pulp, sugar, and lemon zest to the milk. Cover and let the mixture simmer over low heat for about 25 minutes.

Heat the apple juice in a small saucepan; add the apples, cinnamon, and tonka bean (or almond extract) and cook for about 15 minutes until the apples are soft. Serve over the rice pudding. Drizzle honey to taste.

If Boskop apples are not available, another soft variety like Golden Delicious or Pink Lady may be substituted.

*For he satisfies him who is thirsty,
and the hungry he fills with good things.*
—PSALM 107:9

While getting filled up does a favor to the stomach, fasting returns benefits to the soul.

–ST. BASIL

Main Dishes

Fettuccine with Papaya Salad

SERVES 4

Ingredients

2 red chili peppers, minced

4 tsp (20 g) fresh ginger, sliced thin

2 Tbsp sesame seeds, roasted

2 Tbsp sesame oil

8 oz (200 g) tempeh, cubed

Juice of 1 lime

¼ cup soy sauce

⅓ cup fish sauce

Scant ½ cup (100 mL) vegetable broth

7 Tbsp peanut oil

1 tsp agave syrup

2 papayas, chopped

1 cucumber, chopped

2 cups (400 g) konjac (vegan) or regular fettuccine

Sea salt

Black pepper, freshly ground

½ cup (50 g) fresh cilantro leaves

Dried chili threads

Preparation

Mix half of the chili peppers, half of the ginger, half of the sesame seeds, and half of the sesame oil. Marinate the tempeh cubes in the mixture for 15 minutes.

Mix the lime juice with the soy sauce, fish sauce, vegetable broth, remaining chili peppers, remaining ginger, and remaining sesame seeds Then mix in 4 tablespoons of the peanut oil and the agave syrup. Place the papayas and cucumber in a shallow bowl and toss with half of the lime-soy vinaigrette.

Prepare the pasta according to cooking instructions and drain. Mix the hot fettuccine into the papaya-cucumber salad.

In a wok, heat the remaining peanut oil until very hot. Season the tempeh with sea salt and pepper and fry in the hot oil until light brown.

Serve the fried tempeh with the papaya and cucumber salad. Sprinkle the cilantro leaves over the salad. Drizzle everything with the remaining lime-soy vinaigrette and garnish with chili threads, if desired.

Salmon with Green Mashed Potatoes

SERVES 4

Ingredients

12 oz (about half a head, 350 g) cauliflower, divided into florets

¼ cup (25 g) watercress

4 tsp (20 g) butter

12 oz (350 g) starchy potatoes, peeled and cubed

Sea salt

2 shallots, diced

1 red bell pepper, chopped

1 chili pepper, diced

6 Italian parsley stalks, stems removed and leaves minced

2 Tbsp white balsamic vinegar or white wine vinegar

3 Tbsp lemon olive oil*

Black pepper, freshly ground

4 salmon fillets, approximately 7 oz (180 g) each

3 Tbsp olive oil

Preparation

Boil the cauliflower in salted water until it is soft, approximately 5–10 minutes. Blanch the watercress in boiling salted water for about 30 seconds, drain, rinse immediately in cold water, and add to the cooked cauliflower. Puree the cauliflower and watercress with the butter in a blender. Boil the potatoes in salted water until fork tender. Then mash or press the potatoes through a potato ricer into the vegetable puree. Season with sea salt to taste.

Mix the shallots, bell pepper, chili pepper, and parsley with the balsamic vinegar and lemon olive oil and season with sea salt and pepper. Season the salmon with sea salt and pepper. Heat the olive oil in a nonstick frying pan; fry the salmon over medium heat until golden brown on both sides. Serve the fish with the green mashed potatoes and the pepper salsa.

*If you cannot find lemon olive oil, you can make your own by warming (do not allow it to bubble) lemon peels in olive oil for 15 minutes, allowing the oil to cool, then straining the peels from the oil.

Nothing, how little so ever it be, if it is suffered for God's sake, can pass without merit in the sight of God.
—THOMAS À KEMPIS

Lentil and Eggplant Moussaka

SERVES 4

Ingredients

1½ lbs (700 g) eggplant, cut into ¼-inch-thick slices

1 lbs (500 g) tomatoes

2 Tbsp olive oil

2 onions, minced

3 garlic cloves, minced

2 Tbsp tomato paste

½ cup (100 g) beluga lentils*

1½ cups (400 mL) vegetable broth

1½ lbs (700 g) zucchini, chopped

1 Tbsp dried savory

1 tsp ground cinnamon

1 tsp ground cumin

¾ cup (150 g) feta

1¼ cups (250 g) plain Greek yogurt

4 eggs

Sea salt

Black pepper, freshly ground

You may substitute red or French lentils, if necessary.

Preparation

Blanch the eggplant slices in boiling salted water for about 1 minute and rinse with cold water. Drain the slices on paper towels. Wash the tomatoes and remove the stems. Blanch the tomatoes in boiling salted water for about 1 minute and rinse in cold water; then skin them, cut them into quarters, remove the core, and chop them coarsely.

Heat the olive oil in a saucepan; sauté the onions and garlic over medium heat until translucent. Add the tomato paste and the lentils and sauté briefly. Add the vegetable broth, cover, bring to a boil, and simmer gently over low heat for about 15 minutes. Add the zucchini, tomatoes, and spices to the lentil mixture. Cover and bring to a boil again; then simmer over low heat for 10 minutes.

Preheat the oven to 425°F (220°C). Pour half of the lentil mixture into an ovenproof dish and cover with half of the eggplant slices. Pour the remaining lentil mixture on top and cover with the remaining eggplant slices. Mash the feta with a fork and mix with the yogurt and eggs. Season the mixture with sea salt and pepper and spread over the eggplant. Bake on the center rack for about 25 minutes, until golden brown.

Cottage Cheese Frittata with Cucumber and Radish Dip

SERVES 4

Frittata Ingredients

½ cup (250 g) firm boiling potatoes, peeled and diced

½ cup (250 g) zucchini, diced

½ cup (250 g) red bell pepper, diced

8 eggs

1 cup (60 mL) cream

3 Tbsp grated parmesan

1 Tbsp (40 g) fresh rosemary, chopped

Sea salt

Black pepper, freshly ground

1 cup (200 g) cottage cheese

Dip Ingredients

1 cup (200 g) Greek yogurt

1 tsp (5 g) garlic, minced

1 tsp lemon juice

¼ cup (40 g) cucumber, diced

¼ cup (40 g) radish, diced

2 oz (50 g) arugula

Sea salt

Black pepper, freshly ground

Preparation

For the frittata, blanch the potatoes, zucchini, and bell pepper separately in boiling salted water. Allow the vegetables to cool briefly and place in a baking dish. Whisk the eggs, cream, parmesan, and rosemary; season with sea salt and pepper. Spread the egg mixture evenly over the vegetables. Spoon the cottage cheese evenly on top. Preheat the oven to 300°F (150°C). Bake on the center rack for about 40 minutes.

For the dip, mix the Greek yogurt with the garlic, lemon juice, cucumber, and radish and season with sea salt and pepper. Place the frittata over the arugula and garnish with the dip.

Octopus with Vegetable Puree

SERVES 4

Ingredients

3 ½ Tbsp (50 mL) olive oil

2 onions, minced

2 garlic cloves, minced

2 carrots, diced

2 red bell peppers, diced

1 chili pepper, chopped

Sea salt

Curry powder

½ lb (250 g) tomatoes, diced

¾ cup (150 mL) tomato juice

12 oz (350 g) baby broccoli

1 ready-to-use octopus,
approx. 1¾ lbs (800 g), boiled
and chopped

Black pepper, freshly ground

Preparation

Heat half of the olive oil in a pot; sauté the onions, garlic, carrots, bell peppers, and chili pepper over medium heat for about 10 minutes. Season with sea salt and curry powder to taste. Add the tomatoes and tomato juice and cook without a lid until the liquid is completely reduced. Puree the vegetables in a blender.

Blanch the baby broccoli in boiling salted water for 1 minute; rinse with cold water and drain on a paper towel. Heat the remaining olive oil in a frying pan; sauté the octopus briefly while tossing. Add the baby broccoli, sauté briefly, and season with sea salt and pepper. Arrange the octopus on plates with the baby broccoli and the vegetable puree.

For an alternative protein option, substitute the octopus with fried tofu as found in the fried tofu recipe on **pg. 117** *(as pictured).*

"God, having raised up his servant, sent him to you first, to bless you in turning every one of you from your wickedness."
—ACTS 3:26

Eggplant au Gratin

SERVES 4

Ingredients

4 small eggplants

2 Tbsp (30 mL) olive oil

1 onion, diced

3 cups (600 g) peeled tomatoes

¼ cup (20 g) fresh basil, chopped coarsely

Sea salt

Black pepper, freshly ground

1 yellow bell pepper, julienned

1 red bell pepper, julienned

1 zucchini, cubed small

1¾ cups (350 g) feta

Preparation

Preheat the oven to 400°F (200°C). Remove the top stalks from the eggplants. Cut the eggplants in half lengthwise and slightly scoop out the inside. Place the eggplants on the center rack and roast for about 20 minutes. While the eggplant is roasting, take the scooped-out eggplant flesh and cut it into cubes.

In a pot, heat the olive oil; sauté the onion until translucent. Add the peeled tomatoes and let simmer for about 20 minutes. Add the basil and season with sea salt and black pepper to taste. Add the cut vegetables, including the eggplant cubes, to the sauce and let simmer for 10 minutes. Take the eggplants out of the oven and pour the sauce into the hollowed-out eggplants. Finely crumble the feta over the eggplants and put them back into the hot oven on the top rack for 5 minutes.

Renounce yourself in order to follow Christ; discipline your body; do not pamper yourself, but love fasting.
—ST. BENEDICT OF NURSIA

Maluns

4 SERVINGS

Ingredients

1¾ lbs (800 g) starchy potatoes

1 egg

1 ¾ cups (300 g) white flour

Sea salt

Pinch freshly grated nutmeg

1 cup (200 g) butter

Preparation

Boil the potatoes until soft and let them cool. Peel the boiled potatoes and grate them coarsely.

Mix the egg and flour with the potatoes and season with sea salt and nutmeg. In a frying pan, fry the potatoes in the butter in batches, stirring and tossing until golden brown.

> *Maluns is a traditional Swiss dish, originating from the canton of the Grisons.*

"Thus it is written, that the Christ should suffer and on the third day rise from the dead, and that repentance and forgiveness of sins should be preached in his name to all nations, beginning from Jerusalem."
—LUKE 24:46–47

Butternut Squash Quiche

4 SERVINGS

Ingredients

¾ cup (200 mL) milk

1½ cups (300 g) sour cream

5 eggs

1 ½ cup (150 g) grated mozzarella cheese

1 tsp curry powder

1 lb (450 g) butternut squash or pumpkin, grated

Sea salt

Black pepper, freshly ground

1 batch quiche dough (please see doughs on **pg. 191**)

Preparation

In a bowl, mix the milk, sour cream, eggs, grated cheese, and curry powder. Add the grated butternut squash and season with sea salt and pepper. Preheat the oven to 425°F (220°C). Roll out the dough and place it in a pie or quiche pan. Prick well with a fork. Spread the butternut squash mixture over the dough and bake on the lowest rack for about 35 minutes, until golden brown.

If you are able to fast, you will do well to observe some days beyond what are ordered by the Church, for besides the ordinary effect of fasting in raising the mind, subduing the flesh, confirming goodness, and obtaining a heavenly reward, it is also a great matter to be able to control greediness, and to keep the sensual appetites and the whole body subject to the law of the Spirit; and although we may be able to do but little, the enemy nevertheless stands more in awe of those whom he knows can fast.

—ST. FRANCIS DE SALES

Leek Quiche

4 SERVINGS

Ingredients

¾ cup (150 mL) vegetable broth

3¼ lbs (1.5 kg) leeks, sliced into thin rings

Scant ½ cup (100 mL) milk

¾ cup (180 g) sour cream

6 eggs

2 ½ cups (250 g) grated mozzarella cheese

1 tsp (0.5 g) ground saffron

Salt

Black pepper, freshly ground

1 batch quiche dough (please see doughs on **pg. 191**)

Preparation

Heat the vegetable broth in a pot, add the leeks, and simmer until the liquid is reduced. Mix the milk, sour cream, eggs, grated cheese, and saffron in a bowl. Add the leeks, and season with sea salt and pepper.

Preheat the oven to 425°F (220°C). On a lightly floured surface, roll out the dough and place it on a baking sheet. Prick well with a fork. Spread the leek mixture over the dough. Bake on the lowest rack for about 35 minutes, until golden brown.

Through fasting and praying, we allow Him to come and satisfy the deepest hunger that we experience in the depths of our being: the hunger and thirst for God.

—POPE BENEDICT XVI

Spinach Quiche

Ingredients

1 Tbsp olive oil

3 shallots, minced

2 garlic cloves, minced

20 oz (600 g) frozen spinach, defrosted

1¼ cups (250 g) ricotta

1 cup (250 mL) cream

2 eggs

2 cups (200 g) grated mozzarella cheese

Sea salt

Black pepper, freshly ground

¼ cup (50 g) pine nuts

1 batch quiche dough (please see doughs on **pg. 191**)

Preparation

Heat the olive oil in a pan; sauté the shallots and garlic until translucent. Add the spinach to the pan and steam until the liquid has reduced. Let the spinach cool a bit. Mix the ricotta, cream, eggs, and grated cheese in a bowl. Fold in the spinach and season with sea salt and pepper.

Preheat the oven to 425°F (220°C). Line a baking sheet with parchment paper. On a lightly floured surface, roll out the dough. Place the dough on the baking sheet and prick well with a fork. Spread the spinach-ricotta mixture over the dough. Sprinkle the pine nuts on top. Bake on the lowest rack for about 30 minutes, until golden brown.

"Then you shall call, and the Lord will answer;
you shall cry, and he will say, Here I am."
—ISAIAH 58:9

U.S.-Style Flatbread

2 SERVINGS

Ingredients

1 batch Flammkuchen dough (please see doughs on **pg. 191**)

½ cup (100 g) crème fraîche

¼ lb (120 g) celeriac, peeled and grated

Sea salt

Black pepper, freshly ground

⅓ cup (40 g) walnuts, chopped

3 pineapple slices, cut into pieces

Preparation

Preheat the oven to 450°F (240°C). Line a baking sheet with parchment paper. On a lightly floured surface, roll the dough into an oval about ⅛ inch (3 mm) thick and place it on the baking sheet. Spread the crème fraîche evenly over the dough. Spread the celeriac on the crème fraîche and season with salt and pepper. Top with the walnuts and pineapple. Bake on the center rack for about 10 minutes.

And Jesus, full of the Holy Spirit, returned from the Jordan, and was led by the Spirit for forty days in the wilderness, tempted by the devil. And he ate nothing in those days; and when they were ended, he was hungry. The devil said to him, "If you are the Son of God, command this stone to become bread." And Jesus answered him, "It is written, 'Man shall not live by bread alone.'"

—LUKE 4:1–4

Italian-Style Flatbread

Ingredients

1 batch Flammkuchen dough (please see doughs on **pg. 191**)

½ cup (100 g) crème fraîche

Sea salt

Black pepper, freshly ground

2 scallions, sliced into thin rings

¼ cup (40 g) pitted olives, halved

3 Tbsp (20 g) capers

½ cup (50 g) grated parmesan

Preparation

Preheat the oven to 450°F (240°C). Line a baking sheet with parchment paper. On a lightly floured surface, roll the dough into a rectangle about ⅛ inch (3 mm) thick and place on the baking sheet. Spread the crème fraîche on the dough and season with sea salt and pepper. Sprinkle the scallions, olives, and the capers over the crème fraîche. Sprinkle the parmesan on top. Bake on the center rack for about 10 minutes.

Also, temper all your works with moderation, that is to say, all your abstinence, your fasting, your vigils, and your prayers, for temperance sustains your body and soul with the proper measure, lest they fail. It reminds an honorable person that he is ashes and shall return to ashes …

—ST. HILDEGARD OF BINGEN

Vegetable Pie

4 SERVINGS

Ingredients

3 Tbsp olive oil

2 shallots, minced

10 oz (300 g) mushrooms, diced

1 yellow bell pepper, diced

1 red bell pepper, diced

2 Japanese eggplants, diced

1 zucchini, diced

1 cup (200 g) crushed tomatoes

Scant ½ cup cream

Scant ½ cup (25 g) fresh basil, minced

3 Tbsp (10 g) fresh Italian parsley, minced

Sea salt

Black pepper, freshly ground

1 batch pie dough (please see doughs on **pg. 191**)

1 egg, separated

Preparation

Heat the olive oil in a pan; sauté the shallots briefly. add the rest of the vegetables, except the tomatoes, and saute briefly. Then add the crushed tomatoes, bring to a boil, and mix in the cream and herbs. Reduce the heat and season with sea salt and pepper.

Preheat the oven to 400°F (200°C). Using some of the dough, form finger-thick rolls and flatten them along the edge of a 6-cup (1.5 L) ovenproof dish. Add the vegetable mixture to the dish. On a lightly floured surface, roll out the remaining dough to the size of the ovenproof dish to create the top crust. Brush the edge of the dough in the dish with egg white, then place the top crust over the vegetable mixture. Trim the excess dough and press to attach it to the bottom crust. Brush the top crust with the egg yolk and prick the dough several times with a fork. Bake on the lowest rack for about 30 minutes.

"Then I lay prostrate before the Lord as before, forty days and forty nights; I neither ate bread nor drank water, because of all the sin which you had committed, in doing what was evil in the sight of the Lord, to provoke him to anger."

—DEUTERONOMY 9:18

Indian Pie

4 SERVINGS

Ingredients

3 Tbsp olive oil

2 shallots, minced

2 garlic cloves, minced

2 cups (500 g) natural tofu, cut into ¾-inch (2 cm) cubes

1 cup (100 g) chickpeas, cooked

1 cup (200 g) peas, frozen

1 Tbsp curry powder

Scant ½ cup (100 mL) cream

1 tsp cornstarch

Sea salt

Pepper, freshly ground

1 batch pie dough (please see doughs on **pg. 191**)

1 egg, separated

Preparation

Heat the olive oil in a pan; sauté the shallots and garlic. Add the tofu cubes and sauté briefly. Add the chickpeas, peas, curry powder, and cream and bring to a boil briefly. Mix the cornstarch with a little cold water and add to the mixture. Simmer briefly and then season with sea salt and pepper.

Preheat the oven to 400°F (200°C). Using some of the dough, form finger-thick rolls and flatten them along the edge of a 6-cup (1.5 L) ovenproof dish. Add the vegetable mixture to the dish. On a lightly floured surface, roll out the remaining dough to the size of the ovenproof dish to create the top crust. Brush the edge of the dough in the dish with egg white, then place the top crust over the vegetable mixture. Trim the excess dough and press to attach it to the bottom crust. Brush the top crust with the egg yolk and prick the dough several times with a fork. Bake on the lowest rack for about 30 minutes.

When a man begins to fast, he straightway yearns in his mind to enter into converse with God.
—ST. ISAAC THE SYRIAN

Curries

Cauliflower Curry

SERVES 4

Ingredients

1 cup (200 g) red lentils

¼ cup ghee

3 scallions, sliced into thin rings

1 chili pepper, finely chopped

1 tsp ground turmeric

Pinch (.5 g) saffron threads

2 cups (400 g) cauliflower, chopped (about ½ head, including stalk)

4 tomatoes

2 yellow bell peppers, chopped

4 cups (1 L) vegetable broth

1 tsp garam masala

Sea salt

3 stalks fresh cilantro

Preparation

Boil the lentils without salt for 5 minutes.

Wash the tomatoes and remove the stems. Blanch the tomatoes in boiling salted water for about 1 minute and rinse in cold water; then skin them and cut into strips, removing the seeds.

In a pot, melt the ghee; add the scallions and sauté. Add the chili pepper, turmeric, and saffron threads and steam for 2 minutes. Add the cauliflower, tomatoes, peppers, and vegetable broth. Bring to a boil; then cover and let simmer gently over low heat for about 20 minutes. Add the cooked lentils and let simmer for 5 minutes. Add the garam masala and season with sea salt to taste. Serve in small bowls and garnish with cilantro leaves.

Vegetable Curry

SERVES 4

Ingredients

2 Tbsp sesame oil

3 scallions, sliced into thin rings

3 garlic cloves, minced

1 Tbsp hot curry powder

1 red bell pepper, cut into strips

1 yellow bell pepper, cut into strips

2 zucchini, cut into strips

3 Japanese eggplants, cut into strips

2 cups (500 mL) vegetable broth

1 cup (250 mL) coconut milk

Sea salt

Black pepper, freshly ground

Preparation

Heat the sesame oil in a pot; add the scallions, garlic, and curry powder and sauté. Add the other vegetables, sauté briefly, and add the vegetable broth. Boil over high heat for 15 minutes. Add the coconut milk and let the curry boil for another 5 minutes. Season with sea salt and pepper to taste.

Butternut Squash Curry

SERVES 4

Ingredients

2 tsp peanut oil

4 shallots, minced

3 garlic cloves, minced

2 chili peppers, julienned

1 Tbsp garam masala

1 Tbsp ground turmeric

1 Tbsp red curry paste

1 cup (200 mL) vegetable broth

1½ cups (400 mL) coconut milk

1¾ lbs (800 g) butternut squash, cut into
¾-inch (2 cm) cubes

Sea salt

Black pepper, freshly ground

Preparation

In a pot, heat the peanut oil; add the shallots, garlic, and chili peppers and sauté. Stir in the garam masala, turmeric, and curry paste and fry briefly. Add the vegetable broth, followed by the coconut milk. Bring to a boil, cook for 30 seconds, reduce heat, and puree with a hand blender. Add the butternut squash cubes and let the curry simmer over low heat for about 15 minutes. Season with sea salt and pepper to taste.

Chickpea Curry

Ingredients

1¼ cups (250 g) dried chickpeas

2 scallions, sliced into thin rings

3 garlic cloves, minced

2 chili peppers, julienned

⅓ cup (50 g) ground almonds

2½ Tbsp (37.5 g) ghee

¼ tsp ground cardamom

½ tsp ground cinnamon

1 tsp ground cumin

1 tsp ground coriander

1½ cups (400 mL) coconut milk

2 tsp garam masala

Sea salt

Preparation

Soak the chickpeas overnight; then simmer them gently for about 90 minutes, until soft, and drain them. Combine the scallions, garlic, chili peppers, and almonds. In a pot, melt the ghee and stir in the cardamom, cinnamon, cumin, and coriander. Add the almond mixture to the spices and fry for about 2 minutes, stirring constantly. Add the coconut milk and the chickpeas and simmer gently for about 10 minutes. Stir in the garam masala and season with sea salt to taste.

Seafood Curry

SERVES 4

Ingredients

¼ lb (125 g) ready-to-cook shrimp, washed and patted dry

½ lb (250 g) ready-to-cook octopus, washed, patted dry, and cut into bite-size pieces

Sea salt

Black pepper, freshly ground

2 Tbsp ghee

1 onion, diced

3 garlic cloves, diced

1 red chili pepper, minced

2 lemon grass stalks,* outer leaves and upper dry half removed and the light part cut diagonally into thin rings

1½ cups (400 mL) coconut milk

3 kaffir lime leaves,* washed and patted dry

2 Tbsp green curry paste

Preparation

Season the shrimp and octopus with sea salt and pepper.

In a large pan, heat the ghee and briefly sauté the onion, garlic, chili pepper, and lemon grass. Add the coconut milk and kaffir lime leaves and stir in the curry paste. Bring to a boil and let simmer for about 3 minutes. Remove the kaffir lime leaves. Add the shrimp and the octopus and let steep for about 5 minutes. Season with sea salt and pepper to taste.

*For an alternative protein, substitute the octopus with sea bass as found in the Pot-au-Feu-Style Vegetable Stew with Sea Bass recipe on **pg. 77** (as pictured).*

*If these ingredients are hard to find, you may substitute cilantro in place of lemon grass stalks and lime zest in place of kaffir lime leaves.

Snow Pea Curry with Prawns

SERVES 4

Ingredients

2½ cups (600 mL) coconut milk

½ cup (125 mL) vegetable broth

1 Tbsp red curry paste

7 oz (200 g) snow peas, trimmed and cut in half diagonally

½ cup (100 g) frozen peas

14 oz (400 g) ready-to-cook prawns or jumbo shrimp

1 chili pepper, julienned

Sea salt

Preparation

In a pot, boil the coconut milk and vegetable broth. Stir in the curry paste. Add the snow peas and frozen peas and let simmer for about 3 minutes. Wash the prawns, pat them dry, season with sea salt, and add them to the coconut milk mixture. Let the prawns simmer gently for 5 minutes, until cooked. Stir in the chili pepper and season with sea salt to taste.

The WISDOM
of the SAINTS

Fasting gives birth to prophets, she strengthens the powerful. Fasting makes lawmakers wise. She is a safeguard of a soul, a stabilizing companion to the body, a weapon for the brave, a discipline for champions. Fasting knocks over temptations, anoints for godliness. She is a companion of sobriety, the crafter of a sound mind. In wars she fights bravely, in peace she teaches tranquility.

—ST. BASIL, *DE JEJUNIO*, SERMON 1, 6.

Fasting is a kind of wall, then, for the Christian—impregnable to the devil, inaccessible to the enemy. . . . As the Savior says of the devil: "This kind is not cast out except by fasting and prayers." . . . See, then, what the power of fasting is: as much as it offers grace to the one who practices it, it serves as a healing for someone else; while it renders holy the one who observes it, it purifies another person.

—ST. MAXIMUS OF TURIN, SERMON 69.[1]

We should also make our hands fast, keeping them from hoarding and from greed. We should make our feet fast, so that we do not wander through the streets that lead us to see indecent things. We should make our eyes fast, training ourselves not to gaze at beautiful faces and not to search for other hidden attractions.

—ST. JOHN CHRYSOSTOM, *DE STATUIS*, 3.[2]

[Fasting is] lowliness of mind . . . a sacrifice of reconciliation . . . a school of self-control . . . food for the mind . . . [and] good for health.

—ST. AMBROSE, *DE ELIA ET IEIUNIO*, 8, 9. [2]

[1] *Ancient Christian Writers: Sermons of St. Maximus of Turin* (Mahwah, NJ: Paulist Press, 1989).
[2] As quoted in Tessore, *Fasting*.

*Fasting
is a
safeguard
of a soul.*

—ST. BASIL

Breads

Spelt-Nut Bread

1 LOAF

Ingredients

⅓ cup (50 g) white spelt flour

2 tsp (10 g) sea salt

1½ cups (350 mL) water

2 cups (300 g) whole-meal spelt flour

1 cup (150 g) dark spelt flour*

2 tsp (10 g) sourdough starter powder

1 packet (7 g) dry yeast

½ cup (80 g) chopped mixed nuts

4 tsp (20 g) honey

*Type 1100, called *Ruchmehl* in Switzerland, is a dark flour that contains part of the outer grain shell.

Preparation

Mix the white spelt flour and the sea salt in a bowl. In a small saucepan, bring ¾ cup (175 mL) water to a boil. Add the water to the flour and salt in the bowl, stirring vigorously until the mixture becomes thick. Let the mixture cool; then cover it and let it rest in the refrigerator overnight.

After the flour mixture has rested in the refrigerator, combine the remaining dry ingredients in a bowl. Stir the remaining ¾ cup (175 mL) water and the honey into the white spelt flour mixture; then add it to the dry ingredients and knead it into a dough. Cover the dough and let it rise at room temperature for about 90 minutes.

Place the dough on a lightly floured work surface and flatten it slightly. Form the dough into a loaf. Line a baking sheet with parchment paper, place the loaf on the baking sheet, and dust the loaf with flour. Cover the loaf and let it rise at room temperature for 30 minutes.

Preheat the oven to 450°F (240°C). Score the loaf with a knife and bake on the second rack from the bottom for 10 minutes. Then reduce the heat to 400°F (200°C) and bake for about 25 minutes.

"Repent therefore of this wickedness of yours, and pray to the Lord that, if possible, the intent of your heart may be forgiven you."
—ACTS 8:22

Flatbread

6 FLATBREADS

Ingredients

1 packet (7 g) dry yeast

2 ¾ cups (350 g) white flour

2 tsp sea salt

1 tsp baking powder

2 tsp powdered sugar

1 pinch of ground cumin

1 pinch of ground cardamom

Scant ½ cup (100 mL) milk

Scant ½ cup (100 g) Greek yogurt

1 egg

1 tsp tahini

1 tsp olive oil

Preparation

In a bowl, mix the yeast, flour, sea salt, baking powder, powdered sugar, cumin, and cardamom. Add the milk, yogurt, egg, tahini, and olive oil and knead all the ingredients into a soft, smooth dough. Cover the dough and let it rise at room temperature for about 1 hour, until it has doubled.

Preheat the oven to 450°F (240°C). Line a baking sheet with parchment paper. On a lightly floured surface, divide the dough into 6 portions and roll each into a 4- or 5-inch (12 cm) round. Place the loaves on the baking sheet and bake on the second rack from the top for about 4 minutes, until golden brown.

"I despise myself, and repent in dust and ashes."
—JOB 42:6

Spice Bread

1 LOAF

Ingredients

2 ½ tsp (12.5 g) dry yeast

Scant 1 cup (215 mL) lukewarm water

1 ¼ cup (200 g) rye flour

¾ cup (100 g) white flour

2 tsp (10 g) sea salt

2 tsp (10 g) sourdough starter powder

2 tsp (10 g) fennel seed

2 tsp (10 g) coriander seed

1 tsp (5 g) aniseed

1 tsp (5 g) caraway seed

Preparation

Dissolve the yeast in the lukewarm water. Combine the rye flour, white flour, sea salt, and sourdough starter powder; add this mixture to the yeast mixture and knead. Coarsely grind the spices in a mortar. Then add the spices to the dough and knead it briefly. Place the dough in a greased and floured loaf pan, cover it, and let the dough rise at room temperature for about 30 minutes.

Preheat the oven to 425°F (220°C). Bake the bread on the center rack for about 30 minutes, until golden brown.

Fasting is the support of our soul: it gives us wings to ascend on high, and to enjoy the highest contemplation! ... God, like an indulgent father, offers us a cure by fasting.
—ST. JOHN CHRYSOSTOM

Potato Bread

2 LOAVES

Ingredients

Ample 1½ packets (12 g) dry yeast

1¼ cups (300 mL) lukewarm water

4 ¾ cups (600 g) bread flour

2 tsp (10 g) sea salt

1 Tbsp (10 g) dried marjoram

1 Tbsp canola oil

¾ cup (150 g) potatoes, peeled, boiled, and fork-mashed

Preparation

Dissolve the yeast in the lukewarm water. Combine the flour, sea salt, and marjoram and add to the yeast mixture. Add the canola oil and the potatoes and knead the mixture into a smooth dough. Cover the dough and let it rise at room temperature for about 1 hour.

Preheat the oven to 400°F (210°C). Line a baking sheet with parchment paper. Form the dough into two loaves, place them on the baking sheet, and bake on the second rack from the bottom for about 30 minutes, until golden brown.

It is impossible to engage in spiritual conflict, without the previous subjugation of the appetite.
—ST. GREGORY THE GREAT

Low-Carb Rolls

Ingredients

6 eggs

2½ cups (500 g) low-fat sour cream

¼ cup (60 g) sunflower seeds

2 Tbsp (30 g) flaxseed

2 ½ Tbsp (30 g) psyllium husks

1 ½ cup (150 g) oat bran

⅓ cup (50 g) dried cranberries (low sugar)

2 tsp baking powder

⅓ cup (50 g) chickpea flour

2 tsp (10 g) sea salt

1 cup (200 g) mixed seeds

Preparation

In a bowl, carefully mix the eggs with the low-fat sour cream. Add the sunflower seeds, flaxseed, psyllium husks, oat bran, and cranberries and briefly mix. Add the baking powder, chickpea flour, and sea salt and knead with the dough hook of your stand mixer. Let the dough rest for 30 minutes. Pour the mixed seeds onto a plate.

Preheat the oven to 425°F (220°C). Line a baking sheet with parchment paper. Form the dough into 12 rolls and roll each one in the mixed seeds. Place the rolls on the baking sheet and score with a knife. Bake on the second rack from the bottom for about 30 minutes, until crisp.

If we confess our sins, he is faithful and just, and will forgive our sins and cleanse us from all unrighteousness.

—1 JOHN 1:9

Whole Grain Rye Bread

1 LOAF

Ingredients

1¼ cup (200 g) whole grain rye flour

2 tsp (10 g) sea salt

1¾ cups (300 g) cracked rye kernels

2 tsp (10 g) crushed coriander seed

1¾ cups (420 mL) water

1 Tbsp (15 g) sourdough starter powder

1½ packets (10 g) dry yeast

Preparation

Combine ¼ cup whole grain rye flour and the sea salt in a bowl. Bring ¾ cup (150 mL) water to a boil in a small saucepan and stir the water into the flour in the bowl until the mixture becomes thick and sticky. Cover the rye mixture and let it rest in the refrigerator overnight.

In another bowl, combine the remaining whole grain rye flour, the cracked rye kernels, and the coriander seed. Add 1 cup (270 mL) water, the sourdough starter powder, the yeast, and the rye mixture and mix well. Place the dough in a floured baking pan. Cover the pan with plastic wrap and let the dough rise at room temperature for about 24 hours.

Preheat the oven to 400°F (210°C). Remove the dough from the pan and shape it into a loaf. Score the surface several times with a knife, place the loaf on a baking sheet, and bake on the center rack for about 30 minutes.

Then I turned my face to the Lord God, seeking him by prayer and supplications with fasting and sackcloth and ashes. I prayed to the Lord my God and made confession …

—DANIEL 9:3–4

Hot Cross Buns

Hot cross buns are traditionally eaten on Good Friday. The cross etched on the top of the bun symbolically ties it to Christ's crucifixion, while the raisins often used in the recipe symbolize the spices used in the embalming of Christ's body for burial.

There are many stories about the origin of the hot cross bun, but one version recounts that Br. Thomas Rocliff, a fourteenth century monk at St. Alban's Abbey, first baked buns with a cross on top to distribute to the poor on Good Friday.

Hot Cross Buns with Pistachios and Saffron

12 BUNS

Ingredients

3 cups (500 g) white flour

1 tsp (5 g) sea salt

1 packet (7 g) dry yeast

¼ cup (50 g) butter, softened and diced

1¼ (300 mL) cups milk

½ cup (40 g) pistachios, chopped

¼ cup (60 g) honey

Pinch ground saffron

1 egg

Preparation

Mix the flour and sea salt in a bowl. Add the yeast. Add the butter, milk, pistachios, honey, and saffron to the flour and knead into a soft, smooth dough. Cover the dough and let it rise at room temperature for about 90 minutes, until doubled.

Preheat the oven to 350°F (180°C). Line a baking sheet with parchment paper. Place the dough on a lightly floured surface and flatten it slightly. Divide the dough into 12 pieces, 2.5 ounces (70 g) each. Shape them into balls and place the balls on the baking sheet. Using a sharp knife, score them in the shape of a cross. Let them rest, covered, for 30 minutes. Beat the egg and brush the balls with it. Bake on the second rack from the bottom for about 30 minutes.

Hot Cross Buns with Maple Syrup

10 BUNS

Ingredients

Ample 3 cups (500 g) Zopfmehl (braid flour*)

1 tsp (5 g) sea salt

1 packet (7 g) dry yeast

¼ cup (50 g) butter, softened and diced

1½ cups (300 mL) milk

¼ cup (50 mL) maple syrup

1 egg

1 Tbsp milk

Preparation

Mix the flour, sea salt, and yeast in a bowl. Add the butter, milk, and maple syrup and knead into a soft, smooth dough. Cover the dough and let it rise at room temperature for about 90 minutes, until doubled.

Preheat the oven to 350°F (180°C). Line a baking sheet with parchment paper. Place the dough on a lightly floured surface. Divide the dough into 10 pieces, about 3 ounces (90 g) each. Shape them into balls and place them on the baking sheet. Cover the balls and let them rise for about 30 minutes. Whisk/Beat the egg with the milk and brush the buns with it. Using a sharp knife, score them in the shape of a cross. Bake on the second rack from the bottom for about 25 minutes.

Braid flour is difficult to find outside Switzerland. The two most common suggestions for approximating this flour are (1) 10 percent spelt flour and 90 percent wheat flour and (2) 15 percent bread flour and 85 percent all-purpose flour. Alternatively, you can use 3 cups (500 g) of white flour for this recipe.

Hot Cross Buns with Dried Fruit

11 BUNS

Ingredients

Ample 3 cups (500 g) Zopfmehl (braid flour*)

1 tsp (5 g) sea salt

1 packet (7 g) dry yeast

¼ cup (50 g) butter, softened and diced

1½ cups (300 mL) milk

¼ cup (60 g) sugar

½ cup (100 g) dried fruit (raisins, cranberries, or candied ginger), diced

1 egg

1 Tbsp milk

Preparation

Mix the flour, sea salt, and yeast in a bowl. Add the butter, milk, and sugar and knead into a soft, smooth dough. Knead the mixed dried fruit into the dough. Cover the dough and let it rise at room temperature for about 90 minutes, until doubled.

Preheat the oven to 350°F (180°C). Cover a baking sheet with parchment paper. Place the dough on a lightly floured surface. Divide the dough into 11 pieces, about 3 ounces (90 g) each. Shape them into balls and place them on the baking sheet. Cover the balls and let them rise for about 30 minutes.

Whisk the egg with the milk, brush the balls with it, and, using a sharp knife, score them in the shape of a cross. Bake on the second rack from the bottom for about 25 minutes.

Braid flour is difficult to find outside Switzerland. The two most common suggestions for approximating this flour are (1) 10 percent spelt flour and 90 percent wheat flour and (2) 15 percent bread flour and 85 percent all-purpose flour. Alternatively, you can use 2 ½ cups of white flour for this recipe.

Hot Cross Buns with Cornmeal

10 BUNS

Ingredients

1 cup (150 g) cornmeal

Scant ½ cup (100 mL) water

1¾ cups (350 g) white flour

¼ cup (60 g) sugar

¾ cup (200 mL) milk

1 packet (7 g) dry yeast

1 tsp (5 g) sea salt

½ cup (80 g) raisins

1 egg yolk, beaten

¼ cup (50 g) butter, softened and diced

Preparation

In a bowl, mix the cornmeal with the water and let it soak for about 30 minutes.

Put the white flour in another bowl and make a well in the middle. Add the yeast to the well, sprinkle with 4 teaspoons of sugar, and pour in the milk. Mix the yeast, the sugar, and the milk in the hollow to a thin mixture and sprinkle with a little flour. Let the mixture stand for about 30 minutes; then add the rest of the sugar, the rest of the milk, the sea salt, the butter, and the cornmeal mixture. Knead the mixture into a soft, smooth dough. Add the raisins to the dough. Cover the dough and let it rise at room temperature for about 60 minutes.

Preheat the oven to 400°F (200°C). Line a baking sheet with parchment paper. Place the dough on a lightly floured surface. Divide the dough into 10 pieces, about 3 ounces (85 g) each. Shape them into balls and place them on the baking sheet. Brush the balls with a little water and let them rise at room temperature for about 40 minutes. Brush the balls with egg yolk and, using a sharp knife, score them in the shape of a cross. Bake on the center rack for about 30 minutes.

Hot Cross Buns with Rosemary

16 BUNS

Ingredients

6 cups (750 g) dark spelt flour

2 ½ tsp (8 g) dry yeast

2 tsp (10 g) sea salt

2 tsp (10 g) malt extract

Heaping ½ cup (125 g) sour cream

1½ cups (350 mL) water

2 Tbsp fresh rosemary leaves, minced

½ cup (50 g) cranberries

Preparation

Mix the flour, yeast, and sea salt in a bowl. Add the remaining ingredients and knead into a soft, smooth dough. Cover the dough and let it rise at room temperature for about 90 minutes, until doubled.

Preheat the oven to 450°F (230°C). Line a baking sheet with parchment paper. Place the dough on a lightly floured surface. Divide the dough into 16 pieces, about 2 ounces (65 g) each. Shape them into balls and place them on the baking sheet. Brush the balls with a little water and let them rise at room temperature for about 30 minutes. Using a sharp knife, score the balls in the shape of a cross. Bake on the center rack for about 10 minutes. Then reduce the heat to 360°F (180°C) and bake for another 10 minutes. After baking, brush the buns with water to make the surface shiny.

The WISDOM of
HOLY MOTHER CHURCH

POPE CLEMENT XIII, *APPETENTE SACRO,* 1.

Venerable Brothers, you should see that the faithful religiously observe this holy fast, which was recommended by the testimony of the laws and the prophets, consecrated by the Lord Jesus Christ, and handed on by the apostles. The Catholic Church has always preserved it so that by the mortification of the flesh and the humiliation of the spirit, we might be better prepared to approach the mysteries of the Lord's passion and the paschal sacraments.

… It is your duty, Venerable Brothers, to inspire enthusiasm and love of penance in the faithful by word and example.

POPE BENEDICT XIV, *NON AMBIGIMUS.*

At the same time, purified by fasting in the body and in the soul, we prepare to commemorate in a manner more worthy of the sacred Mysteries of our Redemption through remembrance of the Passion and the Resurrection, which are celebrated with the greatest solemnity, especially in the Lenten season. With the fast, almost a mark of our militia, we are distinguished from the enemies of the Church, we turn away the lightning of divine vengeance, and, with the help of God, we are protected in the course of the days from the Princes of darkness.

SECOND VATICAN COUNCIL, *SACROSANCTUM CONCILIUM.*

During Lent penance should not be only internal and individual, but also external and social.… Let the paschal fast be kept sacred. Let it be celebrated everywhere on Good Friday and, where possible, prolonged throughout Holy Saturday, so that the joys of the Sunday of the resurrection may be attained with uplifted and clear mind.

Doughs

Dough for Quiche (Wähe)

Ingredients

2 ¾ cups (350 g) white flour

2 tsp (10 g) sea salt

½ cup (125 g) butter

¾ cup (150 mL) water

Preparation

Mix the flour and sea salt in a bowl. Melt the butter in a small saucepan over low heat. Remove the saucepan from the heat, pour in the water, and add to the flour mixture. Mix the dough with a wooden spoon; then flatten the dough and place it in the refrigerator for about 30 minutes, covered.

Dough for Pies

Ingredients

1 egg

1 lb (500 g) potatoes, boiled, cooled, peeled, and finely grated

1 tsp (5 g) sea salt

1 cup (150 g) white flour

Preparation

Beat the egg in a small bowl and add the potatoes, salt, and flour. Knead into a dough and let it rest for about 60 minutes.

Dough for Flammkuchen (German Flatbread)

Ingredients

1 ½ cup (200 g) white flour

1 tsp (5 g) sea salt

½ packet (3.5 g) dry yeast

Pinch sugar

½ cup (125 mL) lukewarm water

Preparation

Mix the flour and the sea salt in a bowl. In another bowl, dissolve the yeast and sugar in the water. Add the liquid to the flour and knead into a soft, smooth dough. Cover the dough and let it rise at room temperature for about 60 minutes.

ABOUT THE AUTHORS

David Geisser

David Geisser was born and raised in the Wetzikon district of Zurich, Switzerland. David already was an accomplished young chef and published author when he enlisted in the Pontifical Swiss Guard in 2013. He was honored to serve under the 266th Supreme Pontiff of the Church of Rome, Pope Francis. Today, David is one of the leading chefs in Switzerland, author or co-author of seven cookbooks, host of his own TV show, and the founder and leader of the David Geisser Cooking Studio. David and his wife, Selina, reside in Zurich today.

Scott Hahn

Dr. Scott Hahn is an exceptionally popular speaker and teacher, and he has delivered numerous talks nationally and internationally on a wide variety of topics related to Scripture and the Catholic faith. His talks have been effective in helping thousands of Protestants and fallen-away Catholics to (re)embrace the Catholic faith. Dr. Hahn is also the bestselling author of numerous books including *The Lamb's Supper*, *Reasons to Believe*, *Rome Sweet Home* (co-authored with his wife, Kimberly), *The Creed*, *Evangelizing Catholics*, and *Angels and Saints*. He has been awarded the Father Michael Scanlan, T.O.R., Professor of Biblical Theology and the New Evangelization at Franciscan University of Steubenville, where he has taught since 1990, and he is the founder and president of the St. Paul Center for Biblical Theology.

IMAGE CREDITS

The principal photographer and provider of all food photographs is Roy Matter of Zurich, Switzerland. Roy Matter is a food photographer, food biologist, and an accomplished chef himself. Roy Matter and David Geisser have collaborated on three best-selling cookbooks and many other projects. For Roy Matter, his photography work is food art, which is as much a part of the experience as the food itself.

Additional credits

All images are in the public domain unless otherwise noted.

Page X: *Bread Time,* by Eduard von Grützner.

Page 3: *The Sacrifice of Isaac,* by Laurent de La Hyre.

Page 5: *Ezra in Prayer,* engraving by Dore (nineteenth century). Courtesy Lanmas / Alamy Stock Photo.

Page 6: *The Kiss of Judas Iscariot,* coloured engraving from the Heures de Charles d'Angoulême, f. 357, (fifteenth century).

Page 11: *The Butter Tower of Rouen Cathedral,* by Thomas Colman Dibdin.

Page 12: *Disputation of the Sacrament,* by Raphael.

Page 14: *Our Daily Bread,* by Anders Zorn.

Page 16: *Potato-Peeling Girl,* by Albert Anker.

Page 19: *The Angelus,* Jean-François Millet.

Page 23: *Still Life with Bread, Fish and Oysters,* by Peter van Boucle. Courtesy Artiz / Alamy Stock Photo.

Page 25: *Old Woman Saying Grace,* known as 'The Prayer without End,' by Nicolaes Maes.

Page 28: *Crucifixion with the Virgin Mary, St. John and St. Mary Magdalene,* by Anthony van Dyck.

Page 32: *Baking Bread,* by Anders Zorn. Courtesy Peter Horree / Alamy Stock Photo.

Page 35: *To Feed the Hungry,* by Francisco Lopes Mendes.

Page 38: *A Peaceful Sunday,* by Hans Thoma. Courtesy Asar Studios / Alamy Stock Photo.

Page 40: *Jesus Tempted in the Wilderness,* by James Tissot.

Page 43: *Saint Martin Sharing His Coat,* painting in Saint Gatien cathedral. Courtesy Godong / Alamy Stock Photo.

Page 44: *Prayer before Harvest,* by Félix De Vigne.

Page 46: *The Blessing of the Wheat in Artois,* by Jules Breton.

Page 49: *A Cottage Home,* by Joseph Moseley Barber. Courtesy Bourne Gallery, Reigate, Surrey / Bridgeman Images.

Page 50: *Supper of St. Charles Borromeo,* by Daniele Crespi.

RECIPE INDEX

TOPIC INDEX